THE ASYMMETRIC DINGHY BOOK

ASYMMETRIC SAILING FROM START TO FINISH

THE ASYMMETRIC DINGHY BOOK

ASYMMETRIC SAILING FROM **START** TO **FINISH**

Andy Rice

FERNHURST
BOOKS

First published in 2021 by Fernhurst Books Limited

The Windmill, Mill Lane, Harbury, Leamington Spa, Warwickshire. CV33 9HP, UK

Tel: +44 (0) 1926 337488 | www.fernhurstbooks.com

This book contains some content previously published in Andy Rice's *Asymmetric Sailing*, published by John Wiley & Sons Ltd.

Designations used by companies to distinguish their products are often claimed as trademarks. All brand names and product names used in this book are trade names, service marks, trademarks or registered trademarks of their respective owners. The Publisher is not associated with any product or vendor mentioned in this book.

This publication is designed to provide accurate and authoritative information in regard to the subject matter covered. It is sold on the understanding that the Publisher is not engaged in rendering professional services. If professional advice or other expert assistance is required, the services of a competent professional should be sought. The Publisher accepts no responsibility for any errors or omissions, or for any accidents or mishaps which may arise from the use of this publication.

A catalogue record for this book is available from the British Library

ISBN 978-1-912621-34-7

Cover photograph © Tim Olin

Other photographs see p122

Designed & typeset by Daniel Stephen

Printed in Czech Republic by Finidr

ANDY RICE
JOURNALIST, BROADCASTER & CHAMPIONSHIP-WINNING ASYMMETRIC DINGHY SAILOR

Andy Rice has won championships from both ends of a skiff, winning a 49er National Championship as a helm and International 14 Europeans and Prince of Wales Weeks as a crew. He has sailed with a number of top sailors over the years, including Olympic medallists John Merricks, Ian Walker and Simon Hiscocks. Andy continues to race a Musto Skiff competitively in his 50s.

As a sailing journalist, he has reported on every major event from the Olympics to the America's Cup, the Volvo Ocean Race and the Vendée Globe. He writes for many racing-oriented magazines including Seahorse, Yachts & Yachting, Yachting World, Boat International and Sailing World. As a live commentator he has reported at multiple Olympic class events, America's Cup regattas, the Sailing Champions League and the Extreme Sailing Series.

Andy's passion is for asking great sailors what makes them tick and finding out why they're so fast. That was the basis of writing this book, and is also the basis of SailJuice.com, Andy's online treasure trove of top sailboat racing tips, and RoadToGold.net, an online course with top Kiwi coach Hamish Willcox on how to put together a world-class sailing campaign.

The author sailing a Devoti D-One at Lake Garda

THE EXPERTS

There are many friends and experts whose advice I sought when writing the book, some of them quoted, some of them not. From almost three decades of racing in asymmetric fleets like the Laser 5000, the 49er, International 14 and Musto Skiff, I've had the fortune to race with or against some of the best skiff sailors in the business, and I've badgered them for tips and advice along the way. There isn't room to mention everyone I spoke to, but here's a brief background of some of the experts whose advice crops up in the book.

Trevor Baylis, a great crew who has won the 505, International 14 and 18ft Skiff World Championships.

Paul Brotherton, a 49er European Champion from Great Britain, former 470 Olympic representative, and one of the best coaches in the business. He coached the Yngling girls to Olympic gold in Qingdao 2008 and the British 49er team for Weymouth 2012.

Andy Budgen, one of the most talented skiff sailors even if he's not a household name. He's placed 2nd in the 49er Worlds and 18ft Skiffs and coaches many top teams in the 49er class.

Derek Clark, a 470 Olympian, America's Cup designer, and the driving force behind a number of skiff projects including the Laser 5000 and the Rebel Skiff, which features in many of the photo sequences in the book.

Chris Draper, 49er World Champion and Olympic medallist, and America's Cup and SailGP competitor.

Dave Hivey, one of Britain's talents on the small boat scene, having won National titles in the highly competitive RS200 and RS400 fleets as well as the International Moth European Championship.

Steve Irish, a 420 World Champion who moved into asymmetrics and won the RS800 Nationals several times.

Bruce Keen, since winning his first Musto Skiff National Championship in 2010, Bruce has been the dominant force in the trapezing single-hander for a decade, winning multiple World and National titles.

Emma McEwen, 3 times European and twice National Champion in the front of an RS800.

Stevie Morrison, 49er and Fireball World Champion who has twice represented GBR at the Olympic Games.

Chris Nicholson, dominated the 18ft Skiff circuit back in its professional heyday, then won three 49er World Championships. Veteran skipper in the Volvo Ocean Race.

Richard Parslow, a Fireball World Champion, and my coach when I was in the British 49er squad. A goal-setting expert extraordinaire.

Rick Perkins, a Fireball National Champion, but more importantly for this book, a Musto Skiff National Champion.

Frances Peters, ISAF Youth World Champion in the 29er class. She won the girls' fleet, but she probably would have beaten the boys too. A rising star in skiff sailing.

Ben Saxton, World Champion in the Nacra 17 foiling catamaran, represented GBR at Rio 2016 Olympics, multiple dinghy and keelboat champion including six-time winner of the Endeavour Trophy, champion of champions event in the UK.

Mari Shepherd, a top 29er crew, and never afraid of a new challenge, such as when we put her out in the Rebel Skiff for our windy photoshoot.

Chris Simon, rules expert and consultant who has worked at every level of the sport, including the Olympics, America's Cup and Volvo Ocean Race.

CONTENTS

Nathan Outteridge (right) at the Beijing Olympics

I met Andy early on in my asymmetric career at the 2007 49er World Championships in Portugal. This was just after Andy stopped competing in the class, but I have got to know him well since then as one of the leading and most knowledgeable journalist covering high-performance racing.

He has reported on the three Olympics I have competed in and it is obvious when he interviews you that he understands high-performance asymmetric racing. But more than that, he is able to communicate the techniques to the sailing public through his live commentary, written journalism, his sailjuice.com website and, most recently, RoadToGold.net.

I am absolutely delighted that he has written *The Asymmetric Dinghy Book* which includes not only Andy's knowledge but also tips from so many superb sailors. This book will be a treasure trove for anyone who sails an asymmetric dinghy, whether they are just starting to learn about apparent wind sailing or are competing at a high level.

If you want to enjoy asymmetric sailing, and improve your skills, I thoroughly recommend this book. Andy knows what he's talking about. Following his advice will enable you to enjoy being at one with your boat and the wind.

Good luck, and I hope to see you out on the water!

Nathan Outteridge
49er gold (London, 2012) and silver (Rio, 2016) medallist
4 x 49er World Champion
2 x International Moth World Champion
3 x ISAF (now World Sailing) Youth World Champion (1 x 29er, 2 x 420)
America's Cup helmsman in 2013 and 2017

WHO WILL BENEFIT FROM THIS BOOK?

I'm going to assume that you're already familiar with the sport of sailing, and that you've done a bit of racing too. This book is not aimed at the novice, although it is aimed at sailors who may never have sailed dinghies with asymmetric spinnakers before. It is hard to write a book that will appeal to all types of asymmetric dinghy sailor, but in this book you'll discover I've interviewed a range of experts across a spectrum of dinghies powered by asymmetric sails.

We've got tips on how to get the best out of:

- Small hiking dinghies like the RS200 and RS400
- High-performance skiffs such as 49ers and International 14s
- Single-handed asymmetrics like the Musto Skiff and RS700

Even if your particular dinghy isn't directly covered in this book, I really hope you get some great tips from some of the experts we've gathered together, and that you'll be able to carry over some of the hot tips into your own asymmetric sailing.

ASYMMETRIC SAILS + APPARENT WIND = FAST & FUN

To sail successfully with an asymmetric spinnaker – or gennaker – requires you to understand what apparent wind is. Apparent wind is the wind that is generated by the boat moving forwards. It's the same wind as you feel when you stick your hand out the window of a car when the car is moving, or it's the wind in your face when you are cycling. It's artificially generated wind, so you can feel apparent wind even when there is no true wind blowing at all.

Understanding the effect of apparent wind is crucial to sailing with asymmetric spinnakers, but it will also help improve your understanding of all types of sailing. It's easy to think that, on a simple single-handed boat like an Optimist, Topper or Laser / ILCA Dinghy, you run downwind just by presenting the sail to the wind and getting blown along, without any flow across the sail. Indeed, that's how most club sailors do run downwind in

a Laser but ask an Olympic-standard sailor how they steer the Laser downwind, and they're always doing angles, always with flow across the sail. They may be sailing a greater distance, but the increased efficiency by having flow across the sail more than makes up for the extra distance

Unlike a conventional, symmetric spinnaker or the mainsail on a single-hander, the asymmetric spinnaker cannot function without flow across the sail. It is absolutely reliant on wind blowing across the sail. But once you understand this, and that by combining the true wind with the apparent wind generated by your forward motion, then you will discover that you can achieve much greater boatspeed. Many asymmetric dinghies are capable of travelling at least as fast as wind speed and in some extreme cases such as the America's Cup monohulls and catamarans of recent times,

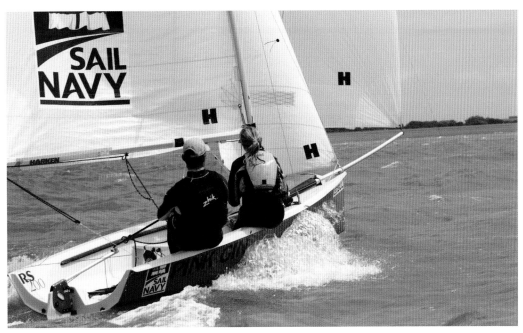

Harnessing apparent wind is the key to fast sailing in asymmetrics

travelling in excess of three times true windspeed is achievable.

One of the fun by-products of asymmetrics is that, for the reasons just given, you can't sail dead downwind – or at least it's very slow and inefficient to do so. Because you want to maximise the apparent wind, you are always sailing angles downwind. Now the run starts to feel similar to an upwind leg, where any sailor knows that it is impossible to sail directly to the windward mark. Well, to some extent the same is true with an asymmetric boat downwind. You have to sail angles, and that makes for a much more tactically interesting and challenging scenario.

However, an asymmetric sail's inability to sail dead downwind is not always a good thing. For example, if you are sailing in confined waters such as in a river or a stream, or you are running close to a shore against an adverse tide, you don't want to have to drive out into stronger tide. So, there are times when you notice the limitations of an asymmetric sail; but most of the time – and certainly in open water – the benefits of an asymmetric far outweigh the benefits of a symmetrical sail. With the asymmetric's superior ability to generate its own wind, it encourages you to start looking for gusts, to

look around for the strongest wind on the water. In a high-performance boat, finding one knot more of true wind speed can help generate as much as two knots more of actual speed through the water.

So, there are very good tactical and strategic reasons for sailing with an asymmetric. In many ways it makes the game more difficult and more challenging but, ultimately, more rewarding when you start to appreciate the tactical and strategic rules of asymmetric sailing.

One of the other benefits of the asymmetric is that, by and large, it is much easier to hoist, gybe and lower an asymmetric spinnaker than a conventional symmetrical spinnaker. It's why, over the past ten years, the majority of beginner and family-oriented boats have come fitted with asymmetric spinnakers rather than anything else.

You have a bowsprit, sometimes fixed but quite often retractable. On many modern dinghies, the gennaker halyard is also connected to a set of blocks which pull the bowsprit out at the same time. So one person pulls just one rope which launches the pole and hoists the sail in one movement. Compare this with a spinnaker where typically, on a two-person boat, it might be the helm who's busy

Handling a gennaker is more straightforward than a traditional spinnaker

hoisting the spinnaker to the top of the mast while the crew is busy connecting one end of the pole to the guy, connecting the centre of the pole to the topping lift, and connecting the inboard end of the pole to the loop on the mast and then setting the spinnaker guy to the right place.

Some people enjoy that challenge, and for many sailors it is one of the fun aspects of crewing. Some would argue that there is a lot of skill in how you get the best out of a spinnaker. The other side of it is that it is much easier to learn how to sail with a gennaker, because you just pull one rope and you're away. In fact, one friend asked me how I could find enough information to fill a whole book on the subject. Yes, at its very simplest, you pull in a gennaker sheet until the sail stops flapping. That's it! End of book!

But the more complicated reality is that while gennakers are very forgiving sails to use, they also tend to be attached to boats that are very demanding to sail and race.

This book is dedicated to helping you get to grips with the wider game of asymmetric sailing and racing. In the process of researching this subject I've spoken to some of the very best in the business. After almost 30 years of racing boats at world-championship level – such as 49ers, International 14s and Musto Skiffs – I thought I knew most of what there was to know, but the asymmetric spinnaker is still a fairly new innovation in the history of sailing and we're learning new tricks all the time. This book condenses the very best of what I've learnt up to now. I hope you enjoy it, and that you find good, solid tips that you can apply to your own asymmetric sailing.

Andy Rice, March 2021

P.S. Throughout the book I refer to 'asymmetric spinnakers', 'asymmetrics', 'gennakers' (half genoa / half spinnaker) and 'kites'. They are all one and the same thing. I try to avoid the term 'spinnaker', reserving that for conventional, symmetrically-shaped spinnakers.

PART 1

THE BASICS

This chapter is about choosing an asymmetric boat and going for your first sail.

CHOOSING THE RIGHT BOAT

It's not within the scope of this book to ask you too many questions about what kind of boat you plan to sail. Because asymmetrics come in many different shapes and sizes, it's difficult to hand out any specific advice, but I just want you to be sure that you've thought about the following factors:

1. ABILITY

Do you have the ability to sail the boat competently? Or, let's put it another way, do you have the potential? Now, I know sailors in their 50s and 60s who handle the 18-foot Skiff and Musto Skiff very competently, and asymmetric boats don't get much harder than that. But even these highly accomplished sailors did a lot of capsizing and swimming before they reached a certain level of competence. Are you prepared to do the same? If so, great! If not, then maybe you want something a bit more stable and easier to handle.

2. TEAM

Are you going to be sailing in a team boat? If so, how much can you rely on your team mate(s) to show up on a regular basis? Better to agree on the goals and the schedule for the year before you put down your hard cash on a boat.

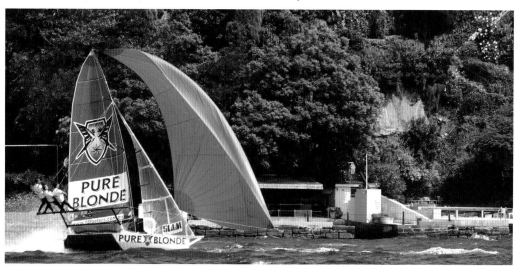

The 18-foot Skiff is great fun if you know what you're doing, but it will bite you if you don't!

3. BUDGET

Do you have the money, not just for the boat, but for its upkeep and maintenance? If you're racing a boat where you expect to be doing a lot of capsizing and putting the equipment through quite a bit of abuse while you drag yourself up the learning curve, then it may be better to do your learning on a well-sorted second-hand boat. Even better if you can get the seller to throw in a day's coaching to help you get to grips with the basics. It's also a great way to check that the boat you're buying is working properly and that you haven't been sold a pup.

4. LOCAL FLEET

Is there a local fleet at a nearby sailing club, or a good racing circuit that you can get involved in? While any new boat is exciting to sail initially, the novelty will eventually wear off. But it's the racing and the camaraderie that will keep you interested. So give this factor some serious thought before deciding which boat to sail.

APPARENT WIND SAILING

GOT TO GET UP TO GET DOWN...

One of the difficult things to get your head around when you're discovering asymmetric sailing for the first time is the idea that if you want to get downwind you need to head up first. In planing conditions, if you want to get the bow pointing as low as possible downwind and make the best VMG (Velocity Made Good) to the next mark at the bottom of the course, then the way to do that initially is actually to luff up as high as possible towards the wind. Unless you do this, you're not really apparent wind sailing, you are just wafting downwind with the breeze and the gennaker will be caught behind the mainsail and the jib, and will never get a chance to fill properly. So, if you're new to this, the first thing to do is to head up perhaps more than you think you need to, and get the air flowing across the gennaker from luff to leech and drafting out the back of the sail.

Once you do that, the apparent wind will kick in and start building on itself. As the apparent wind increases, it also moves forward, and you need to sheet on the gennaker and the mainsail to compensate. And, if it's windy, you'll need to hike out as hard as possible to counteract the increase in power. In strong winds you'll find those who hike out hardest actually end up sailing lowest and deepest towards the leeward mark. At first it doesn't seem to make sense. After all, in most sailing you sit in to sail lower, but not in an asymmetric when you've got the power of apparent wind on your side.

HOW LOW CAN YOU GO?

In light-to-medium airs, when there isn't enough wind to get the boat planing, then it's about sailing as low as possible before you experience a massive drop off in flow across the sails. Where sailing dead downwind is an option in non-asymmetric boats, it's never an option with asymmetrics. You always need to sail angles downwind, and in light-to-medium conditions the trick is finding out just how low you can go.

On a keelboat you may have electronic GPS equipment which you can use to help determine your best VMG downwind. On a dinghy, you don't have that luxury, so you have to develop a feel for

To create your apparent wind, first you need to luff up to build the speed

when you think the boat is travelling at the optimum VMG downwind. Quite often you can't really work this out until you start racing other boats, when you can compare yourself to others nearby. In marginal planing conditions you'll find there are those who like pushing high and sailing extra distance for the extra speed, while there are those who like really running deep and going slower, but sailing a shorter distance to the next mark.

Both those extremes have their place, and sometimes it pays to do a little bit of each. A lot of the time, the decision that you make about whether to sail in high, medium or low mode is based on the tactics of where the boats around you are, and where you're aiming for next. It is also based on where you think the best breeze is. Sometimes, when you're in a nice but narrow line of breeze, it pays to sail low to stay in it as long as possible. The temptation can be to head up, get on the plane and sail really fast – only to sail yourself out of the breeze line.

So it's really important to be able to sail in all these modes. We'll address this in the Boatspeed chapter. And it's also important to know how and when to apply these modes on the race course, which we'll address in the Racing: Strategy & Tactics chapter.

Two International 14s sailing in very different modes

Ben Saxton: Learning about VMG in asymmetrics

Although he was a very good Optimist sailor, downwind Feva sailing was initially a mystery to Ben:

> *Downwind was one of my super-strengths in the Optimist, but the first time I got into an asymmetric boat – an RS Feva – I just couldn't get anywhere near this kid who was a couple of years younger than me, James Peters. I was 13 or 14 so it was pretty hard being given a lesson by this kid who wasn't even a teenager! It took me quite a long time to learn that I need to luff the boat up to push higher and get the breeze flowing across the sail. You've got to get that balance right between not sailing higher than you need, but not sailing so low that you lose the power out of the asymmetric. But the mistake that I made, not heading up enough early, I think that's a common one for newcomers to asymmetric sailing.*

Frances Peters: Getting to grips with asymmetrics

Former ISAF Youth World Champion in the 29er, Frances Peters, looks back at her move into asymmetrics from conventional dinghies:

> *It was a big transition to make at first, because suddenly you're sailing big angles downwind. There's so much more to be gained and lost, so it was a big mental transition and you had to start thinking about it from a new perspective. Upwind we get used to watching pressure [the wind] coming down and sailing to the pressure and sailing on the lifted tack. You've got to start thinking in a similar way downwind. But it's another perspective downwind because you're actually sailing away from the pressure, so you've got to watch where the pressure's going and you've got to try to find ways to stay in the pressure as it moves. Equally it's easy to ignore shifts downwind and you should try to pay more attention to them as well.*
>
> *I've found that having got some experience in asymmetric sailing, going back into a symmetrical conventional spinnaker or a boat without a spinnaker at all, it really helped my sailing. It really made me think a lot more about what was going on around me, and there's so much to be gained and lost downwind as well as upwind. Before asymmetric sailing, I used to think that places weren't really gained or lost downwind and that actually it didn't really make much of a difference which way you went. But as you start sailing in asymmetrics, you realise that there's so much else going on around you. It highlights the difference in pressure and shifts across the course, and although it's not as obvious in other types of sailing, it still applies. Sailing asymmetrics makes you much more aware of the possibilities downwind.*

GETTING THE BASICS RIGHT

HOISTING FROM A CHUTE

If you're using a boat with a spinnaker chute then it's the crew who tends to do all the hoisting in a two-handed boat. Because the halyard is usually connected to the bowsprit launch mechanism, the head of the gennaker and the tack all go out at the same time. One rope does the whole job of hoisting, which is why it's a one-person task. This means the helm is free to steer the boat so that it's upright and stable and gives the crew plenty of opportunity to hoist the spinnaker without worrying about helping to keep the boat upright.

HOISTING FROM A BAG

With a boat where the gennaker is hoisted from a bag, you might want to share out the job of hoisting the sail, as there are more ropes to pull. It's a matter of dividing up the workflow in such a way that you get your gennaker up and pulling in the shortest amount of time after the windward mark. For example, maybe it makes sense for the helm to pull up the spinnaker halyard while the crew pulls out the pole and the tack line. Try a few combinations of tasks until you find the one that achieves the hoist in the quickest time.

Despite the enormous sail, the 18-foot Skiff gennaker is launched and retrieved into a bag

In a boat with three or more crew, such as an 18-foot Skiff, then you can divide up the workload even more. So the typical work pattern might be:

- Helm continues to steer while taking the mainsheet from the middle man
- Forward hand goes to leeward to prepare the gennaker by opening up the bag; he then pulls out the bowsprit; at the helmsman's command the forward hand hoists the gennaker and cleats it off
- While the forward hand is hoisting the gennaker, the middle man pulls the tack line until the tack reaches the end of the bowsprit; he then moves straight to the kite sheet (taking it from the helm if the helm has already picked it up) and gets the kite set while the forward hand sets the jib and tidies the cockpit and the kite halyard in particular

RIGGING THE GENNAKER

When you rig the gennaker, make sure you get it right before you go afloat! I can guarantee that at some point in your asymmetric sailing career, you will forget this simple advice. Some lessons you have to learn for yourself, and believe me, there are few more embarrassing or painful than having to re-rig the gennaker out on the water. It's not easy, and it often results in a capsize. You can remind me of this fact the next time you see me up on the foredeck of my Musto Skiff!

Have a set routine for rigging the boat, and you'll avoid foul-ups on the water

If you launch from bags, as with a B14 or an 18-foot Skiff, then at least all you have to do is tie three corners to the correct rope. But for the sake of simplicity and avoiding silly errors, make sure you write 'Tack', 'Clew' and 'Head' on the correct corners. And I'd tie them on in that order too, although this isn't too critical. One reason for doing this is for rigging up on a windy day, when you don't want to have the kite blowing around the dinghy park and potentially capsizing your boat. Having the names written on the corners means you can have the kite stuffed in the bag and still tie on the corners without exposing too much sail to the wind.

Now, if you launch from a chute, which is the norm for most asymmetric dinghies, then you have the added complication of a retrieval line, which is basically the other end of the halyard because it's one continuous line. The retrieval line makes it much more possible to create tangles and to get it wrong if you're not careful with your rigging procedure. It also makes it much harder to re-rig it on the water if you get it wrong, so it's particularly important to make sure that you've got your rigging correct with a chute style of boat.

There are different ways of doing it, but my favourite way of rigging a gennaker on an International 14 or a 49er for example, is to:

- Tie the tack first, with the bowsprit retracted into the boat
- Loop the kite sheets through the clew and reeve the port sheet through the port-hand ratchet block on the boat
- Pull the foot of the sail tight so that you know there's no tangle – I do this on the port side of the boat on the 14 because this is the side where the kite hoists from
- Take the retrieval line (already threaded through the spinnaker sock) and run it underneath the foot of the sail, and then run it through the bottom retrieval patch near the foot
- Depending on whether you've got a one-, two- or three-patch retrieval system on your kite, make sure that the halyard is going through all the correct patches, and then tie the end of the retrieval line off to the top retrieval patch

- Take the other gennaker sheet that runs around the starboard side of the boat, take this starting from the clew, and run it along the side of the boat inside the gennaker, making sure it goes over the top of the retrieval line, runs around the forestay and then back down the other side of the boat through the ratchet block
- Tie off your gennaker sheets in the middle of the cockpit
- Finally, tie the halyard on to the head of the kite

The reason for attaching the halyard last is so that if the wind does catch the sail while you're rigging it, you're not going to get it filling and flying out from the top of the mast, potentially capsizing the boat

ADDING A SPACER KNOT TO THE RETRIEVAL LINE

If you've got a kite with two or three patches, then the sail can bunch up at the chute mouth as you're pulling it back into the boat during a kite drop. This can sometimes create extra friction and effort for the crew at a crucial point in the race. One way to avoid this is to thread a plastic ball on to the retrieval line which sits between two of the patches. If you tie a figure-of-eight stopper knot or a long bowline, and create a gap of, say, 10cm (4 inches) between the patches, this will help avoid the bunching effect as you haul the kite back into the chute.

Yellow retrieval line is tied with a long bowline to keep the patches apart as they go into the chute

and causing damage while you are on the shore. So the gennaker halyard is always the last thing to be tied on and then you're ready to fully retract the kite into the chute and that should make sure that you don't have any tangles. If it's windy you can pull most of the sail into the chute before you attach the halyard.

If the winds are light, and you don't think it's going to cause any harm to the boat, then take the opportunity to double check your rigging. Hoist the gennaker to the top of the mast and make sure that all the sheets are running clear. If the winds are strong, the chances are that you won't get an opportunity to do that, which means that when you get out on the race course, unless it really is extremely windy, you want to check that you rigged the gennaker correctly as early as possible before the start of the race. If by any chance you have made a mistake, you at least give yourself the maximum time to put it right. But good luck!

HEALTH & SAFETY

There's some safety gear and clothing you might want to take with you, particularly if you're sailing a high-performance boat for the first time. Take a knife, in fact take two. I keep one in my buoyancy aid tied to a lanyard, and I keep a diver's knife on the back bar of the Musto Skiff. It doesn't happen often, but every few years there is a story of a sailor who got tangled up with the rigging or caught under the boat, and a knife might just have made the difference to whether they lived or drowned.

Knife. Take a knife, and wash it in fresh water after every time you sail so that it stays sharp and ready for action.

Spares. Take a shackle key, some spare shackles and a spare piece of rope. You'll be surprised how often you need them, and how much easier life becomes when you have them at the ready.

Wear gloves. If you're sailing an asymmetric boat properly, you're moving sheets all the time, and that can wear out your skin really quickly. If you're steering a 49er or other skiffs where the crew is playing the mainsheet upwind, then you might get away without gloves, but pretty much every other job on an asymmetric boat requires gloves.

Builders' gloves are cheap and have a great grip

Helmets. I've never worn one but I've certainly thought about it, particularly for those days where I'm out on the open sea in my Musto Skiff by myself. When you're learning and expecting a bit of crash and burn, a helmet will give you a lot more confidence to take risks. It will help speed up your learning curve.

Foot loops. These are vital bits of kit on high-performance trapeze boats and can be as simple as a piece of hose pipe with some rope running through the centre, to ready-made windsurfer foot straps to specially made sailing foot loops. It's really down to personal preference. Some are designed to give way if they're subjected to a lot of force. The idea is that, if you have a big tumble, the foot loop detaches before it causes damage to your foot or ankle. It doesn't happen very often, but people have occasionally been known to break an ankle when they get their foot stuck after falling off the boat in a capsize. So it's important to get some foot loops that you have confidence in using.

Footloops should be stiff enough to stand upright for easy access

GOING SAILING FOR THE FIRST TIME

Tempting as it might be to launch your new boat the first time, be sure to pick the right conditions, particularly if you've chosen a boat that is more high performance than you've been used to. Just bear in mind your level of experience and don't give yourself too much to do the first time you go out sailing.

If you possibly can, find someone who's already got experience in the boat to go sailing with you the first time. It will massively shorten your learning curve, and could help you avoid some costly errors.

A great shortcut to better boat handling from day one, is to do some shore drills. Tie the boat down very securely to the shore – on its trolley or on some tyres – and anchor the boat side to side to the ground so that it's firm enough that you can actually sit on board the boat and you can walk around it, and sit down from one gunwale to the other. If it's a trapeze boat, you want to be able to trapeze off the side of it and you can work out a lot of your routines,

Shore drills are a great way of building up muscle memory and hand-eye coordination

your foot movements and your hand movements without having the added challenge of worrying about keeping the boat upright. If you're going to be dry-land trapezing, tie an anchor rope around the mast at hounds height and secure it side to side, so that you can get out on the trapeze knowing that you're not going to capsize the boat on top of you!

Now, you might think that you look like a beginner doing this, and maybe you do! But some of the best sailors, including top Olympic medallists taught themselves the basic manoeuvres on shore with the boat tied down in the boat park. This enables you to learn all the foot and hand movements many, many times in a safe environment. It's a great way of building up muscle memory and hand-eye coordination, ingraining good habits from the very start without the risk of capsize, breakage or injury.

Once again, the process becomes even more valuable if you can find somebody who already has more experience of sailing that kind of boat than you do. So, get them to show you what they do, invite

Double check everything before you go afloat

them to go for a walk around the boat and show you the different things that they do through various manoeuvres. It's also a good way of practising and improving your sailing on a day when there's no wind, or there's too much wind to safely go sailing. A good way of making use of what otherwise would be wasted sailing time.

Once you feel that you've got those drills for all

the various manoeuvres worked out – the main ones being tacking, gybing, hoisting and dropping the gennaker – then pick a day, a light-to-medium air day to go sailing for the first time. Again, if you've got the option to sail with someone with some experience as opposed to maybe the person who's going to be your regular crew or helm, then take the experienced person because you'll learn so much more about how to do things right first go. You'll probably end up breaking less gear, capsizing less, feeling more confident in the boat much sooner if you've learnt from someone else who's been through the learning curve already. You can then take that experience with you back into the boat when you start sailing with your regular sailing partner.

One of the most important things that you need to be able to do safely, is to hoist and, particularly,

lower the sails. That should be your first drill, to hoist the gennaker, making sure that it's rigged correctly once it's been hoisted, setting the gennaker and then lowering the gennaker again. Once you've done that then you can try experimenting with some gybes, sailing the boat at different angles with the gennaker hoisted trying a very deep run and trying a tight reach provided it's not too windy, just getting comfortable with how the gennaker works and how it responds to different sailing directions.

SAFE LAUNCH & RECOVERY

Have a set routine for launching, and give yourself more time than you think you need

LAUNCHING FROM A LEE SHORE

One of the most challenging parts of sailing high-performance boats is launching them off the shore, particularly if the wind is blowing directly on shore, the dreaded 'lee shore'.

If you're sailing a double-handed boat, then the crew (or whoever's biggest and strongest of the two) should hold the boat in the water by the windward shroud, while the other sailor takes the trolley back to the beach, and then hops into the boat to get the board and rudder down as much as

possible in the depth of water available.

Then, as the crew gets ready to hop into the boat, the helm should have tiller in hand and get the jib half-sheeted, ready to pull the bow away from the wind. As the crew jumps in, avoid the temptation to get away from the shore as quickly as possible – i.e. don't try to point into the wind. This will almost certainly stall the boat and you'll most likely blow back onto the shore.

Instead, get the jib pulling and feel what the forces are on the rudder. Only pull in the mainsail if

Musto Skiffs launching from a lee shore – note the windward heel to keep the boat sailing in a straight line with half the board and rudder down

you feel lee helm in the rudder, i.e. you are having to push the rudder away. On the other hand, if you're feeling weather helm, pull on some more jib and heel the boat slightly to windward. All the while the crew wants to gauge the depth of water and get the board fully down as soon as possible. The same goes for the helm and the rudder, but don't do this at the expense of losing control of the boat. Keeping the boat going in a straight line and avoiding the stall remains the highest priority until you are safely away from the shore.

LAUNCHING FROM A WINDWARD SHORE

If you're launching from a windward shore, things get easier, although if you're sailing a high-powered skiff then the bear-away can, in itself, be quite a challenge in strong winds. In this case, get the rudder halfway down, but launch with the daggerboard / centreboard fully up. Although the boat will be slightly tippy, provided you're aware of this fact, you'll be fine and you'll drift sideways out into deeper water. Then, once you're away from the

shore, put the daggerboard in / centreboard down, get the rudder fully down, and then start sailing.

LANDING ON A LEE SHORE

If you're coming into a lee shore, it's often worth dropping the mainsail before you come in. Do this at least 50 metres (50 yards) offshore – possibly more, depending on how long you think it will take to get the main down and safely stowed in the cockpit. If it's particularly windy, you might even want to furl, lower or unhook the jib from the sheet, as you'll be amazed how quickly you approach the shore even with a small amount of sail area.

LANDING ON A WINDWARD SHORE

As you get within jumping out distance of the shore, raise the board and rudder halfway, and the crew should be ready to jump out and get wet at least up to the waist, possibly up to the neck if you've misjudged your approach!

But generally this is simplest of all the launching and recovery manoeuvres.

First let's look at all the standard moves you need to know in order to get around the race course. We'll cover some of the more fancy stuff later. Mainly we'll be focused on using the asymmetric sail downwind, but we do need to know how to manoeuvre the boat all the way round the course. So before we head downwind, let's take a brief look at tacking upwind.

TACKING

From close-hauled on one tack

Initiate the turn and begin to roll the boat

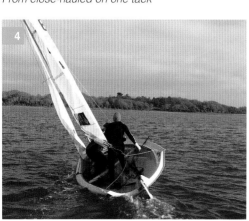

Once through head-to-wind, begin to cross the boat

Sitting smoothly on the new windward side

Tacking on most asymmetric dinghies is not radically different to any other boat of similar ilk. There's not much that needs altering on a hiking dinghy – you would roll tack as you would any other medium-perfomance dinghy (see below).

But lightweight skiffs (see p26), particularly with self-tacking jibs, do require some thought about technique.

Firstly, aim for a flat boat throughout the manoeuvre. Don't try to roll tack the boat, as you'll never cope with the power and acceleration you already have. When the battens on a fully-battened rig pop through to the new tack, you already have a power surge to cope with and, if anything, you want to exit a tack slightly heeled to windward so that you come upright as the battens pop.

If you've got a self-tacking jib, most likely it will be the crew taking the main through the tack. If it's off-the-boom sheeting, most crews prefer to pass the mainsheet behind their back as they move through the boat.

For the helm, the most important thing is to steer slowly but consistently through the tack on to the new course. Don't slow down too much, or else the boat will lose momentum and stall. But don't oversteer, otherwise you'll struggle to cope with too much power, especially if the jib is still sheeted in hard.

Easing the jibsheet a few inches before the tack will give you a bit more room for error until you get the hang of the tack.

WIRE-TO-WIRE TACKING

Wire-to-wire tacking looks great, and it's not as hard to do as it might look as Emma McEwen demonstrates in the RS800 (see p27).

If you've got your handles set to the right height, then you can hang on a straight arm, which doesn't require too much strength. If you're sailing a twin-trapeze boat, it's great if the helm can do this too, but it's not absolutely essential, it's just the icing on the cake.

However, it is very useful for the crew to be able to reliably wire-to-wire tack – and gybe for that matter – as it gives the helm a lot of confidence in being able to steer all the way through the manoeuvre on to the new heading, knowing that the weight of the crew will be there to counteract the power surge as the sails fill on the new tack. It makes the manoeuvre a lot more predictable and safer.

With practice, the crew should be able to hook up on the new side while hanging on to the handle and also holding the mainsheet. But, in the early days, it's OK to hand the mainsheet over to the helm until the crew is hooked on and settled.

Some single-handed trapeze sailors in the RS700 and Musto Skiff like to wire-to-wire tack and gybe, but this is a high-risk option, as there's no second pair of hands to help out if you start struggling to juggle tiller, mainsheet and trapeze handle.

Much better to practise a more predictable manoeuvre where you get your body weight on the new rack, settle on the new heading, and then get out on the trapeze.

Rolling more to windward as you turn

So you are sailing normally on the new tack

PART 1

26

LIGHTWEIGHT SKIFF TACKING

Andy Budgen and Mari Shepherd come off the trapeze as they at the start to tack

They move through the boat in unison, matching their speed to the speed of the boat tacking

Maintaining a flat boat throughout the turn

As they exit the tack, Mari picks up the mainsheet with her aft (now left) hand, while Andy allows a little windward heel

With the boat flat throughout the tack, and safely on the new heading, they can take their time getting hooked on to their trapeze wires knowing that they're safely through the tack.

And power up on the new tack

WIRE-TO-WIRE TACKING

From trapezing on the beat

Move up towards standing

So both of you are standing

Begin to move across the boat

Duck under the boom

Move towards the other side

The crew step onto the rack

Onto the outer rack

And out on the wire again

GYBING WITHOUT THE GENNAKER

One of the benefits of travelling fast downwind with the gennaker is that the force of the wind as you go through the gybe is fairly small, particularly in planing asymmetric dinghies. Let's say you're sailing in 15 knots of breeze and moving through the water at about 11 knots meaning you've only got a soft 4 knots of apparent wind wafting across the deck. The boom will almost float across during the gybe, none of the slamming from one side to the other that you get on slower boats. This means that when you don't have the gennaker, you actually miss that extra speed of going downwind. You're back in the more familiar territory of conventional boats, of having to cope with a much greater force on the boom when the boom gybes.

You still need to be able to know how to gybe without the gennaker, whether it's for the manoeuvres in the pre-start, or if you've got to take a 360° or a 720° penalty. If you have to do this in a strong breeze, the 'no-gennaker' gybe is about the hardest manoeuvre you can do, so it's well worth practising a drill outside of racing.

The other areas where gybing without the kite can help during a racing situation are at a windward mark where you might want to gybe immediately onto port gybe to get into a fresh line of breeze on that side of the course. Or it might be that there's a raft-up at the leeward gate and you have to get the gennaker down early – in which case you'll have to gybe without it.

There are even extreme situations in 49er World Championships where teams have actively decided not to hoist the gennaker because they pretty much know that they're going to capsize on the gybe, whether they're flying the gennaker or not. They take the view that if you're going to capsize, it's going to be quicker to get the boat upright again with just main and jib, and not having to worry about getting the gennaker back in the chute first. So they were going for two-sail gybes and hoping for the best, and if they got through it upright, then that was a bonus.

GYBE WITH PACE

So how do you do it? As with any gybe, the key to a successful no-gennaker gybe is to go into the gybe with as much pace as you can and to maintain that pace as much as possible all the way through the gybe. If you're in a trapezing boat, ideally it means staying on the trapeze for as long as possible on a power reach, sailing as fast as you can with the righting moment available to you. So if you're in a hiking boat, hiking as hard as you can and then, as you steer into the gybe, try not to let the main out too much. Because the more that you let the main out, the further you'll have to turn through the breeze when you come out of the manoeuvre on the new gybe.

Better if you can keep the mainsail two-thirds in and then, as the boom starts to swing across, you

Sail into the gybe with as much speed as possible…

And you have a much better chance of staying upright

have a bit of mainsheet that you can ease to soften the blow of the boom slamming across. Also, if one of you can grab the boom and haul it across the centreline just before it gybes of its own accord, it reduces the amount of steering required.

The problem with waiting for the boom to cross by itself is that you need to steer higher for this to happen, and the higher you sail out of the gybe, the more prone you are to broaching. So, do whatever you can to convince that boom to get across sooner than it would like.

If you're sailing a boat with two or more people, you need to aim to coordinate getting your weight from one side to the other with your weight in the middle of the boat for the minimum of time. Move from fully hiking on one gybe to fully hiking on the other gybe as quickly as possible.

In moderate-to-strong winds, you won't need to apply any roll to your gybe. You want to be flat all the way through the manoeuvre, possibly even slightly heeled to leeward on a very high-speed high-wind gybe. If in doubt about how quickly to get your body weight across to the new windward side of the boat, do it sooner than later. Do it too late and the boat will fall in to windward. Do it too early and you'll let the boat heel to leeward and you probably won't make it through the gybe at all, but you'll broach and capsize on the gybe that you were already on. Eight times out of ten, though, the reason why people capsize on windy two-sail gybes is because they've moved their body weight across too late.

If you're sailing a trapeze boat and you've got your teamwork well worked out, the crew should run straight for the new trapeze handle and jump straight out on the new gunwale of the boat. This means the helm can confidently steer high out of the gybe to take advantage of the extra righting moment.

If the crew doesn't manage to take the jib through with them on this manoeuvre and the sail flaps, that's OK. At this stage of such a difficult manoeuvre, crew weight and balance of the boat is more important than setting the sails. You can sort that out after you've safely got through the manoeuvre.

Too much heel going into the gybe...

Can make it tricky to recover from

If you're not confident of being able to get a lot of crew weight onto the new side quickly, then the helm needs to steer more of an 'S' shape out of the gybe, such as you do on slower boats, where you steer the first half of the 'S' to get the boom across. As soon as you can feel the boom moving across and about to slam on to the new gybe, you do the second part of the 'S' to bear away the boat back on to a dead downwind or very broad reaching angle, so that the boat stays underneath the rig. In that sense, gybing an asymmetric skiff is no different to gybing any other kind of sailing boat. It's just that a lot of asymmetric boats with their fully battened and over canvassed rigs, require that bit more precision. That's why making the most of your crew weight as quickly as possible is the key to surviving a difficult gybe.

Nice and flat for this gybe, but get ready to bear away again the moment the boom flips across

HOISTING THE GENNAKER

Hoisting the gennaker is something that you should attempt for the first time only in light-to-medium airs. Hopefully you'll have already done your shore drills, so you've got some of your routines worked out between the helm and the crew. Here are some of the basic roles and responsibilities of each of the sailors during the hoist.

Most championship race courses are based on port-hand rounding, which means that you'll be bearing away from a beat onto a starboard reach or run before hoisting the gennaker.

So sail upwind normally. The helm needs to tell the crew to get ready to bear away. If any controls need easing at this stage then do so. These may be easing the cunningham and the vang and, keeping the boat nice and flat, you ease the main and the jib together and bear the boat away onto quite a deep broad reach so that the crew can come in off the trapeze.

At this point, keeping the boat upright becomes the helm's responsibility, creating a level and steady platform for the crew to be able to pull the halyard and hoist the gennaker, which on many boats also pulls out the bowsprit. The more stable the boat, the less the crew needs to worry about anything else and he or she can focus on hoisting the gennaker as quickly and efficiently as possible.

Once the gennaker is hoisted the crew should join the helm on the windward side gunwale (provided there's enough wind) and start sheeting on the gennaker sheet. The helm may also need to head up at this point, to get the gennaker filling properly, so heading up from a broad reach onto a slightly tighter reach, until the sail sets. At the moment when the sail does fill, then the boat will lurch forward with the acceleration. As the apparent wind builds, the boat will lean over, so you will need either to hike it down or bear away – or most likely a combination of the two – so that you're heading lower and the boat remains upright.

Stevie Morrison and Ben Rhodes bear away around the windward mark

When borne away and stable, Ben goes in and Stevie keeps the boat upright

Ben starts pulling the halyard to launch the bowsprit and hoist the gennaker

As soon as the kite reaches the top, Ben picks up the leeward gennaker sheet…

Gets the gennaker setting as he goes out on the trapeze handle and hands the gennaker sheet to Stevie until he's got safely hooked on

Then Ben takes back the sheet and both sailors lower themselves on the wire for more righting moment

OUTHAUL? LEAVE IT OUT

Once you're up and running at full speed, check that cunningham has released properly, that the vang is set, and ease the outhaul if necessary. On most high-speed asymmetrics easing the outhaul makes little difference and is just one more thing to remember to pull on at the leeward mark. So, unless you really think it's going to make a noticeable difference, leave the outhaul in its upwind position.

DAGGERBOARD / CENTREBOARD

Leave the daggerboard / centreboard down. Whatever position you have it for upwind, 99% of the time it will be just right for going downwind. The gennaker moves the centre of effort of the sail plan forwards, so you need the lateral resistance of the board for the sail plan to work against. There is one example where you might want to raise the board in light winds, as one of our experts, Dave Hivey, will explain later on (p87).

COMMON MISTAKES
Don't Come In Too Soon

Too soon? The crew needs to make sure the boat is safely downwind before stepping into the boat to start the hoist

Bear Away, No Really Bear Away!

A common mistake with the hoist is for the helm not to have borne away enough, so that when the crew starts hoisting the kite, there's a danger of the kite filling halfway up, which then makes the job of finishing off the hoist much more difficult and also increases your chance of capsizing. So it's vital to make sure you've done a deep enough bear-away. This will help keep the gennaker in the wind shadow of the mainsail, which means that it's easier to hoist because there's less wind resistance for the crew to work against.

It is possible to bear away too much, but this doesn't happen very often, but you'll know about it when you've done it, because you'll capsize. That's the only limitation of sailing too deep. There are good tactical reasons for sailing deep at this point in a race as well, but we can come on to that later.

Picking Your Moment In Waves

Another golden rule is that, if you're sailing in waves, make sure that you pick your moment before the crew runs forward to start the hoist. Fast skiffs frequently outrun the waves – even without the gennaker hoisted. Timing is everything. Wait until the bow has ploughed through the back of a wave and make sure that there's going to be sufficient time to get the majority of the hoist completed before the bow goes into the back of the next wave.

Make sure a wave isn't going to give you a nasty surprise mid-hoist!

Smooth Systems, Strong Arms: The Key To A Fast & Safe Hoist

The crew's responsibility is to be able to hoist the gennaker smoothly and quickly and, if the boat is well rigged and everything is running smoothly, then a fit crew should be able to arm-over-arm hoist, i.e. their body is more or less still, they're standing up in the middle of the boat and each arm is alternating, going from being down by the halyard block to going up above the crew's head before the next arm takes over and does the same action.

The crew grabs the halyard from down by the halyard block

And then pulls all the way with that hand before starting again with the other hand

Sometimes, if the gennaker fills halfway up, or if it's waterlogged and heavy from a nose-dive or a capsize, then 'arm-over-arming' a hoist is not going to be possible. Instead, grab the halyard with both hands and with straight arms and, most importantly, a straight back, and use your knees to do the hard work. Basically, adopt the same position as a weightlifter about to lift a heavy weight. Obviously, this is a lot slower, but at times it's the only option available to you to complete the hoist. The risk is that the slower the hoist, the more vulnerable you become to the gennaker flopping into the water off the leeward side of the boat, and then trawling the gennaker. That's when the real trouble begins, but we'll save that for another chapter!

TIPS FOR HOISTING FROM A BAG

When you're hoisting from a bag, make sure that the gennaker halyard is forward of the spreaders (and definitely not hooked around the windward spreader!). The crew should be constantly checking this upwind and particularly before the windward mark. On the bear-away, keep the boom slightly off the shroud so that the mainsail has no chance of squashing the kite halyard and gennaker against the shroud and the leeward spreader.

Hoisting from a bag can be very prone to ending up in a trawl – with the gennaker falling in a clump, straight from the bag and over the side into the water, resulting in a very rapid deceleration as the fleet sails past you!

After passing the windward mark

Bear away and move into the centre of the boat

The helm pulls out the bowsprit and the crew hoists the kite

Before settling into their normal positions

Tips To Avoid The Trawl

Keep the boat flat or even slightly heeled to windward during the hoist. Heeling to leeward leaves you more prone to trawling.

Co-ordinate the launch of the tack line so that it follows the hoisting of the halyard. If the halyard is going up slowly for any reason, then the tack line launch needs to be delayed too. Ideally the two corners of the sail should hit their targets (i.e. the halyard block at the top of the hoist and the end of the bowsprit) at the same time. But the progress of the tack line launch should never be ahead of the halyard's progress up the mast.

If you DO trawl, luff the boat up into the wind, take off all the speed, and then the crew goes to leeward and retrieves the soggy sail back into the bag.

PART 1

Dave Hivey: Hoisting in hiking boats

"**The bear-away** – *The crew should never ever go in for the hoist until the boat's fully borne away. With light winds it's very easy, you just bear away. When it gets breezy it becomes a little bit more critical on the timing. The crew should never go in until I say 'OK', which is just after the boat starts to bear away. Once it starts to go, that's fine. If the crew goes in too late, then it might actually capsize to windward although that doesn't happen very often. More often you see people going into the boat too soon before the bear-away has begun.*

The hoist – *To do a fast hoist the crew needs to be on his or her feet, so they can hoist hand-over-hand without ever missing the halyard. Which means that, if the hoist goes wrong, it's the helm's fault because he or she hasn't given the crew a stable platform. So when I bear away I'm always looking to keep the boat plumb upright all the way through the hoist.*

If there are no other boats around us, I'll be looking to go as low as possible to make the platform as stable as possible. I'll drop right down, and I will bring my body weight in as well. If we're going round with lots of boats, then sometimes I have to make sure that the kicker [vang] is all the way off. I don't ease the main too much to make sure that it's not powered up too much. I hike out pretty hard if I have to hold my height to make sure we stay high while the crew is doing the hoist but, again, it's really important that you keep that stable platform even when you're trying to hold height for tactical reasons.

You can see Mari Shepherd and me showing you what to do in this photo sequence on a windy and wavy day in an RS200."

Make sure the boat is level as you bear away

When safely borne away, Mari stands up to start hoisting…

She grabs the halyard, but a big wave threatens a nose-dive, so I hike as far back as possible…

Leaving Mari free to continue hoisting

The bow comes out of the wave

As Mari completes the hoist, she picks up the gennaker sheet and gets ready to join me on the windward side

EXPERT ADVICE

Bruce Keen: Hoisting in single-handed skiffs

"Make sure you've fully completed the bear-away manoeuvre before attempting the start of the hoist. The cunningham and vang should be fully eased and the boom out near the leeward shroud.

If you're in big waves, pick your moment and, if necessary, wait! At this point you're steering with the end of the tiller hooked under your leeward knee with your windward knee kneeling on the windward side of the cockpit for stability. Once you're sure you can complete the six or seven armfuls of hoisting required before the bow hits the next wave, start hoisting as quickly as possible because this is the moment when you're most vulnerable to a gust or a big wave.

If you find that you're ploughing straight into the back of the waves on starboard, it might be worth gybing on to port where you'll be sailing across the waves and less likely to nose-dive. You can also pull the head of the kite out of the chute, while you are waiting for a flatter patch of water, as it will reduce the number of armfuls required when you find an opportunity to hoist.

Having the correct length of halyard will also help you with a fast hoist. You want it to be long enough that you can grab big armfuls without feeling restricted. But the halyard mustn't be so long that the retrieval line is at risk of hooking under the bow while you're charging downwind.

It's useful to have a mark on the halyard near the cleat so you know when the kite is fully hoisted. Grab the tiller extension, sheet in the kite, sheet in the mainsheet, hook on to the trapeze and get the speed on."

When stable Jamie Hilton starts the hoist

The kite is going up as he reaches the spreader mark

Passing the spreader mark the kite is almost up

The kite is beginning to fill as he leaves the mark behind

EXPERT ADVICE

Emma McEwen: Hoisting in trapeze skiffs

Preparation – *Take care rigging the kite. This is the most common part of boat rigging to get wrong in the haste to launch. Allow enough time to rig calmly and double check what you have done. There will be a lot of kite to handle and it's a physical job to hoist and drop, so make things as easy as possible with good set-up:*

- *Having the right length of kite halyard and a good elastic take up will make hoisting and dropping easier and reduce the risk of tangle and knots as you pull on the line*
- *Ensure all the blocks in the system spin freely and keep them well rinsed with fresh water after sailing in salt water*
- *Tape up or use bicycle inner tube to cover any sharp edges or split rings or shackles that might snag the kite*
- *Use a lubricant to help the pole slide in and out with less friction*

Typically, the downhaul end of the spinnaker halyard will attach to a couple of points on the sail. Setting the tail end bowline to a longish length will keep the two eyelets apart as they are pulled into the chute and so spread the size of the bunched area of the kite so it can fit more easily into the chute.

Some physical fitness will be very helpful, best generated by lots of time on the water pulling the kite up & down!

Hoist – *Before the bear-away make sure you know whether you will be gybing or not around the windward mark or spreader mark. The helm will usually make that call depending on boats around you and where the wind is likely to be best on the run.*

In any decent breeze, it will not be possible to get the boat to bear away unless you have released the kicker and cunningham in advance. Do this as you approach the windward mark or on the spreader reach if there is one. Calibrate the kicker so that you can let it off the appropriate amount ready for the run. Allow time if you have had the controls on to max as the loads will be high; raise yourself up on the trapeze wire to get better angle on the lines to the cleats if need be. Try to do this efficiently as you will be losing boatspeed all the time, but you must release the controls before the mark.

Once the call is made to hoist, your sole aim is to get the kite up & set as fast as possible; ideally faster than the crews around you. This requires focus and aggression if you want to win!"

LOWERING THE GENNAKER

When you want to lower the gennaker, always give yourself more time than you think you need. You'll particularly start noticing this when you start racing against other boats and you'll find that the leeward mark often comes up quicker than you expect. You'll need even more time if you're dropping into a bag.

There's nothing worse than dropping the gennaker too late. Much better to drop it just a little bit too early and have a bit too much time to get ready for the rounding rather than not enough. So, on a standard drop, the crew can either just drop the spinnaker sheet or, if you want to keep the speed on for a little bit longer, the crew can pass the sheet to the helm who'll hold it in his front hand, whilst the crew goes forwards to drop the gennaker.

DROPPING INTO A CHUTE

Standing over the halyard one foot either side, the crew releases the spinnaker halyard at the cleat and starts catching the rapidly falling gennaker by arm-over-arm dropping, pulling on the retrieval line in front of the retrieval block, and behind the cleat if your boat is set up this way. Doing this, you are unlikely to let the halyard re-cleat on the way down.

You'll find the drop a lot easier than the hoist, because gravity's doing a lot of the work for you, so you'll find the first bit of the drop very easy. As soon as the crew starts this first piece of the drop, if the helm is still holding the sheet, they should release at this point and then, as the first retrieval patch comes round the forestay and goes into the mouth of the chute, this is when it gets harder. If you have the strength, you still keep on arm-over-arming. If not, revert to the weightlifter's stance – straight arms, straight back – and use your knees to do the last few pulls to get the gennaker safely tucked away with the head of the sail just disappearing at the end of the final pull.

As with the hoist, keeping the boat upright and stable is all down to the helm. You are unlikely to need to change direction that much during the drop, because you'll have already been sailing fairly deep anyway, but really all you're doing is looking to keep the mast dead upright, above the boat, making it as easy as possible for the crew just to focus on getting the gennaker safely stowed.

SMOOTH RUN PAST THE FORESTAY

If you find that the kite is particularly hard to get in because it's bunching up on the forestay, remember that tip for putting a spacer knot between two of the kite patches (see p19). Also, if class rules permit, you might want to put a piece of plastic tubing on the lower few feet of the forestay to give the kite a smoother run.

EXPERT ADVICE

Dave Hivey: Dropping kites in hiking dinghies

As you approach the leeward mark, make sure you're coming in a little bit high, giving yourself the ability to bear away before you go for the drop. You don't want to be too powered up as the crew goes in for the drop because it makes the boat quite difficult to keep stable at that point. If you can come in just slightly above the layline it gives you the option to bear away and take the power out of the sails. There's nothing wrong with doing bit of a bear-away and coming back up to the mark again as long as you are really careful about not opening your transom to other boats looking to get room on you at the mark. But, as with the hoist, it's vital to give the crew that nice stable platform.

As you're about to drop the kite, there are two things you can do; either the crew passes the kite sheet back to the helm, or the crew can stand on the sheet so they keep the kite filled that fraction longer. It also means that the kite is not allowed to flap, so it is far less likely to be twisted for the next hoist. And it also keeps the sheet taut, discouraging it from looping around the bow and possibly falling over the front and getting stuck underneath the boat, which can happen on the RS200 and 400.

As with the hoist, Mari stands up to speed up the drop...

… and Mari completes the drop as I steer to round the leeward mark

Andy Budgen: Dropping kites in two-man trapezing skiffs

Andy has borne away and stays in the back foot loop to keep the bow out while Mari works on getting the kite back into the chute...

Mari works arm-over-arm to pull the gennaker down

Note how far back Mari is standing, helping Andy keep the bow out; if she had to get this into a bag, a nose-dive would be a greater risk than it is here...

With the kite safely back in the chute, Mari joins Andy on the trapeze, ready to put maximum righting movement on the windward rack before Andy rounds up for the beat

Bruce Keen: Dropping kites in single-handed skiffs

There's a lot more to be lost by dropping too late rather than dropping too soon. The only exception is in light winds with the current pushing you upwind, when you might want to hold on to the kite until the very last moment before rounding. Under normal circumstances, and particularly when it's windy, a lot of sailors get caught out dropping too late. A great opportunity for you to pounce!

In the Musto Skiff a lot of people like to begin the gennaker take-down by sheeting in the kite hard behind the mainsail which is now eased out to the shroud. This chokes the power out of the sail and really slows the boat down which makes it more manageable while you're steering with the tiller under your leeward knee.

But I like to use the leeward mark roundings as an opportunity to overtake boats and I try to keep the boatspeed going throughout the manoeuvre. So I uncleat the halyard first, and then rapidly oversheet the foot (before it falls in the water). I then start pulling in the retrieval line as quickly as possible and it is a very fast manoeuvre when done correctly. But it is also more high risk, so practise it first before trying it in competition.

If I've got time, I'll try to pull on the cunningham before the rounding but don't bother with the vang. The most important goal is to have a high exit out of the leeward mark, and once you've secured that, you can sort out the vang and other stuff once you're going upwind.

This Musto Skiff sailor has got his kite bagged nice and early, leaving him clear for a controlled mark rounding

DROPPING INTO A BAG

Dropping into a bag requires good timing, otherwise there's a danger of dropping the gennaker in the water and trawling it.

The helm first needs to bear away close to a dead run, taking all the apparent wind and pressure off the gennaker. The crew will then have less of a fight on their hands to get the sail past the windward side of the jib and into the bag. For the manoeuvre the crew should stand behind the bag next to the windward shroud. First release the tack line and gather most of the foot and start stuffing it into the bag. Release the kite halyard and arm-over-arm the kite into the bag as quickly as possible. If you have a retractable bowsprit, make sure the bowsprit slides back into the boat to minimise the chance of hitting any other boats during a congested mark rounding.

What if you have overstood the layline for the leeward mark and don't have the space to bear away on to a dead run? On smaller asymmetrics it's still possible to get the kite down on the windward side, but you need to be fast. While the helm (or another crew member) still has the kite sheeted on, the forward crew person grabs the lazy windward sheet. Then the crew releases the halyard and tack line in quick succession and the kite will fall very quickly towards the water. But, if you're fast, the crew can haul in on the windward kite sheet and, provided you get the clew of the gennaker past the forestay and on to the foredeck, you're pretty much safe from there. Just keep on hauling the kite in around the forestay and stuffing it in the bag as you go. It's not pretty, it feels risky, but it's easier than it sounds. Provided you've got a fit heart and fast arms you won't have a problem.

The crew uncleats the halyard

Then gathers the foot of the kite

And pulls the kite down

Packing it into the bag

GYBING WITH THE GENNAKER

The rules for a successful gybe are very simple: keep it fast and keep it flat. Let's look at the components of a good asymmetric gybe.

NOT TOO MUCH RUDDER!

Gybing the gennaker is very different to gybing on a single-sailed boat or even on a boat with a conventional spinnaker. What takes most people by surprise is how little the boat needs to be turned to get through the gybe, particularly when you're travelling at speed. One of the big mistakes for newcomers to asymmetrics is for the helm to use far too much rudder and to make too much of a handbrake turn through the gybe. In medium-to-strong airs too much rudder can result in you capsizing. Using small amounts of rudder has a big effect compared with gybing other kinds of boat.

KEEP IT FLAT

The other difference from conventional dinghies is that it's much more important to keep the boat flat throughout the manoeuvre. There's little need for roll gybing, except in the very lightest of breezes. If you attempt a roll gybe in anything stronger, again you're probably going to end up capsizing. You won't go too far wrong if you can keep the boat flat all the way through the manoeuvre.

YOUR FIRST ASYMMETRIC GYBE

First I'm going to assume that you've already done some dry-land practising, working through your

Keep the boat as flat as you can during the gybe

footwork, body movement and hand movements, and that, as helm and crew, you've made a plan as to how you're going to gybe.

Also, don't give yourself the challenge of learning to gybe in a force five! Choose a light-to-medium breeze when you try things out for the first time.

So, here goes. As you're approaching the gybe the helm needs to make sure that there's space behind and to leeward before you begin changing course. You must make sure there are no other boats in your way and that you have a clear space to gybe into, because the direction changes are so much greater compared with conventional kinds of boat when they gybe.

Once you know that you've got space to gybe, tell the crew to get ready to gybe. If they're on the trapeze (hang on, what are they doing on trapeze? This is your first gybe! One thing at a time, please), this might mean that they come in off the trapeze first so that they're in a position to move through the boat as the gybe begins.

As the boat bears away, move your body weight to the centreline, keeping the boat flat so that, as the power in the rig decreases, so too does your righting moment. As the boom gybes across the middle of the boat, you should have reached the middle of the boat, with your head below boom height!

As the boat exits the gybe and gets on to its new course, crew weight should move smoothly and quickly to the new windward side of the cockpit, about the same time as you expect the boom to complete its arc and for the mainsail to start setting on the new side.

In full-power conditions, where you're using maximum righting movement downwind, the ideal gybe is one where you spend the absolute minimum time in the middle of the boat. You want to be full hiking (or trapezing) on one gybe and into full hiking / trapezing on the new gybe with as little downtime as possible. Not only is this fast, it's safer too. Lightweight asymmetric dinghies are like bicycles. Both are hard to keep upright when they're stopped or travelling slowly.

Andy Budgen and Mari Shepherd hadn't sailed the Rebel Skiff before, so this isn't a bad first attempt at a gybe

As they come off the trapeze, Mari keeps the kite filling for maximum speed into the gybe, and note how little the tiller moves from the centreline…

A bit of windward heel creeps in, and it would have been better to keep the boat flat or even slightly heeled to leeward

Also, the kite is starting to billow out the front and would have been better if Mari could hold on to the old kite sheet for longer…

Andy eases the boom to the shroud to keep the boat on its feet, but at least they're safely through the gybe with a flat boat

Andy swaps steering hands as Mari hauls on the new kite sheet…

With the kite filling on the new gybe and the boat accelerating…

Andy and Mari hook up on the trapeze and get moving to full pace again

TWO TYPES OF GYBE: 'BLOW-THROUGH' OR 'PULL-THROUGH'?

There are two ways the crew can manage the gennaker through the gybe. Here we'll call the two versions the 'blow-through' gybe and the 'pull-through' gybe.

Blow!

The blow-through involves holding on to the old sheet through the gybe and keeping the gennaker sheeted in its old position until the wind on the new windward side of the boat is blowing the kite against the jib and forestay. At this point the crew releases the old sheet and rapidly sheets on with the new gennaker sheet. If you do it quick enough, you can snap on the new sheet and the kite will fill instantly on the new gybe.

This works particularly well on boats with long bowsprits such as the International 14, where the kite has a nice big space to blow past the forestay. It does not work so well on boats like the 49er with a short bowsprit, making the gennaker prone to sticking against the jib, particularly if the kite is wet and old. Newer kites with their slippery finish tend to blow through much more nicely than older ones.

Blow: From one gybe

Keep the kite filling

Don't release the sheet

So the kite backs

And half blows through with some help from pulling the sheet

To pop on the new side

Pull!

The pull-through gybe involves the crew starting to haul on the new sheet as you begin the gybe manoeuvre. As the boom is gybing, the clew of the kite should be coming past the forestay and, by the time you're onto the new course for the new gybe, the kite should be in place and already setting on the new side.

When you get the timing right, the pull-through gybe is very fast and efficient, requiring less steering to get the flow re-attached on the gennaker. But it requires more physical effort and more timing to get it right.

Which?

So, which is best? In the majority of cases, the blow-through gybe will serve you very well. It requires less effort and less timing to get it right, but if you find the kite is sticking to the jib, it might mean it's time to shell out some money on a new one. You should still practise the pull-through gybe too, though. It is the best light-wind option, as we'll explain in the next chapter.

TIMING YOUR MOVE

Whilst you're learning the timing of all of this, there's even something to be said for getting to the new side a little bit sooner than you think you need. Better to get there too early than too late. The mistake that many people make is to get there too late, resulting in the boat gybing (a good thing) but capsizing almost immediately afterwards (a bad thing).

On the other hand, if you go through the boat

Pull: Cleat jib on the new side

Release old spinnaker sheet

Pull in the new spinnaker sheet

To fill the spinnaker on the new gybe

Pull the boat upright

Start sailing on the new gybe

too early, this can mean that the boat slows up too quickly and you never end up actually completing the gybe. The boom will never actually cross the centreline, which means that you might broach and capsize to leeward on the old gybe. This error tends to be the less frequent of the two so, if in doubt about your timing, move your weight over to the new side sooner than you think you need to.

You'll soon gain in experience and confidence, and feel ready to start gybing faster.

In planing conditions you can even gybe with the boat slightly heeled to leeward all the way through the manoeuvre. If you think about it, that's exactly what a windsurfer does when he's powering through a carve gybe. The mast is always pointing away from the sailor (to leeward) and it's almost as though the tip of the mast is fixed in space, with the board rotating around the tip of the mast. Fast asymmetric dinghies respond to the same treatment.

Dave and Mari at full pace as they prepare to gybe the RS200...

Dave and Mari keep the boat nice and flat through the gybe

At one point it looks like a bit of windward heel is going to creep in...

They swiftly correct with a combination of steering...

And bodyweight faster up to the new side of the boat...

Dave has been steering with his hands behind his back, and finally swaps hands for the new gybe

THE POWER OF THE BATTENS

For sailors used to sailing conventional dinghies with soft sails, the surge of power created by an asymmetric dinghy can come as a shock. Part of the reason for this is that most modern asymmetric boats are equipped with powerful, fully-battened mainsails. When these stiff battens flick at the end of the gybe, they create a power surge that needs to be counteracted, and that's why there's an added incentive – compared with older more traditional boats – to get your weight onto the new side a little bit quicker. If you leave it too late, the power of the 'batten flick' can result in you capsizing, but if you get your timing right, you can harness the 'batten flick' to help accelerate you up to full speed on the new gybe.

Andy catches the boom before it slams across – this takes the 'oomph' out of the sail and reduces the slamming moment that would occur if he just let the boom fly across unchecked; when the battens in the mainsail flick to the new side, it creates a power surge just when you don't want it – at least not in heavy winds – Andy's controlled release of the boom minimises the slamming force

THE MEASURE OF A GOOD GYBE

We've already stressed the importance of travelling as fast as possible through the whole gybing manoeuvre. You know you're gybing really well when the boom seems to float from one side to the other through the manoeuvre. In strong winds this is one of the sweetest differences between gybing a conventional boat – where the boom nearly always slams from one side to the other – and a fast asymmetric. Even if the wind is blowing 18 knots, if you're gybing with 12 knots' boatspeed, there's only 6 knots of force moving the boom across. This is a great way of gauging your progress with gybing. The more the boom 'floats', the better you're gybing.

COMMON MISTAKES

Remember the two 'F' words: Flat and Fast.

The speed that you turn the boat needs to be matched by the speed you move through the boat. If you can't move that fast, don't turn so fast!

If you're managing to gybe but capsizing immediately afterwards, chances are you turned the boat too quickly or didn't move through to the new side of the boat quick enough. Either slow down the rate of turn and / or move through the boat more quickly.

If you capsize before even completing the gybe, chances are you've slowed down too much and the pressure in the mainsail has become too much to handle. Remember that asymmetric dinghies are like bicycles – unstable at low speed. So, first make sure you're travelling as close to maximum speed before beginning your gybe. If that by itself doesn't solve the problem, try increasing the rate of turn with the rudder and keep your crew weight hiking out as long as possible before starting the gybing manoeuvre.

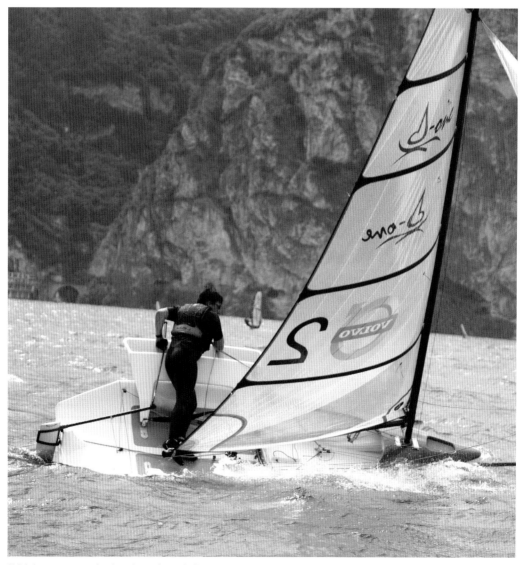

Which common mistakes have I made?

EXPERT ADVICE

Dave Hivey: Gybing hiking asymmetric dinghies

The helm should be the one to initiate the gybe, as they're the one doing the tactics and making the decisions downwind. I'll try to give the crew warning if possible. Sometimes, if a boat around us gybes, I'll literally just have to say, 'We're going'. But let's say we've got an ideal situation where we're going to pick a spot on a wave. I'll ask, 'Are you ready to go?' The crew will basically say, 'Yes!' or 'No'. If it's a 'Yes!', I start to initiate the gybe as the crew starts to go in. As the crew starts to go forward I will then lean out and start to initiate the gybe to make sure it's got some windward heel on the way in, which will start with an ease of the mainsail. I then go for my gybing strap (a grab rope hanging from the centre of the boom) and pull it across nice and early – a lot earlier than you'd think. As I gybe I'll pull the gybing strap across and then hold it in the middle for a second just to make sure it doesn't slam out onto the far side, and then slowly ease it out as I cross to the other side with my body.

The key move next is to bring the boat up onto the breeze on the new gybe depending on where the crew is. If the crew spent too long in the front because he or she didn't get the kite sheet, fell over, or anything that might have happened in the gybe, then you need to hold the boat in that stable downwind phase for a bit longer before you come up. If you see the crew hit the new side with the kite sheet, then we can start to heat it up a lot more. I'll vary the speed of the gybe depending on where the crew is, and that makes the gybing an awful lot safer. The crew keeps the old sheet where it is, sometimes even snapping it on a little during the gybe. Then, when the kite backs against the jib, the crew releases the old sheet with one hand and, with the other, snaps on the new sheet as the kite blows through to the new gybe. When you get your timing right, there's very little effort involved and the kite fills instantly, making it safe and fast.

Dave and Mari let the boat heel to windward a little too much for these windy conditions, but...

Dave pulls the boom to the centreline as they start to cross over...

... Good control of the rudder and the mainsail on the exit means they get away with it

As they both move to the new windward side

And they are back on an even keel and going fast again

EXPERT ADVICE

Emma McEwan: Gybing two-man trapeze skiffs

Go for the handle

Bend your legs

Move into the cockpit

Kite blows through

Step onto the new rack

Hook on

EXPERT ADVICE

Rick Perkins: Gybing single-handed skiffs

> *Ideally you need three or four hands to gybe an asymmetric single-handed trapeze boat like the Musto Skiff. But, assuming you don't, the key is to develop and learn a process that you then go out and try to implement. If you kind of try to make it up as you go along as you're bouncing down the water at high speed, it's very hard to work out what to do next unless you have a clear plan in the first place.*

> *If you learn what you're trying to achieve through shore drills, through studying videos on YouTube or through photo sequences, you've got a much better chance of actually executing a good gybe than if you are just making it up as you go along. So have a clear set of processes and practise them in your head and on shore before trying it on the water.*

> *It's vital to keep the speed on as you approach the gybe. It's very easy to come in off the wire and sit around and start fiddling around with your bits of string. While you're doing this, the boat is slowing and the rig is loading. So once I've made the decision to gybe, I'm taking the slack out of the windward kite sheet and, depending on the wind conditions, I might ease the main slightly. Not a lot, just a little bit such that it's not quite so pinned in once I've got through to the new gybe. As you're about to start turning into the gybe, take the slack out of the windward kite sheet, trim the mainsail out if needed, come in off the wire, bear away gently and cross the boat early – possibly even before the boom has gybed. If you watch a video of a good sailor gybing in slow motion, you'll see that they are stepping through the boat on the inside of the turn, getting on the new side before the boom has crossed.*

> *As soon as the boom comes across, give the new kite sheet an enormous pull, what is known in the Musto Skiff fleet as the 'Superman punch'. So you're picking up the new sheet from the windward ratchet block and pulling it across your body in one big long pull to try to get the spinnaker around on to the new side as quickly as possible. Sit down on the new wing so you've got a bit of weight on the new side with the boat still going fast. If you get the Superman punch right, hopefully the kite is filled on the new side. If not, sheet in until the kite fills, settle down, hook on, out you go on the wire, and sheet the mainsail back in for maximum boatspeed.*

Gybing a single-hander, the mainsail needs to stay cleated in a 'safe' position while the helm focuses on steering and gybing the gennaker

Musto Skiff World Champion Richard Stenhouse uses the 'Superman punch' to pull the kite around the forestay and through to the new gybe

'PRE-GYBING THE MAINSAIL'

I like to pull the boom across using the boom strap. If you wait for the boom to cross in its own time, when it does gybe, you'll never beat it to the new side. If you wait for the wind to catch the new side of the mainsail and blow the boom across, it will just slam across to the new side. You'll have no chance of matching that power surge with your body weight on the other side when it hits the new side.

If you pull it across slightly earlier than that point, you'll find that there's almost no power in it when you pull it across. You can just slowly pull it over your head and then ease it out on the new side, and there'd be no power at all. And remember to slow the boom down as it runs out to the new leeward shroud.

When it's windy, I'll oversheet the main a little bit because that reduces the power in the mainsail (because you're presenting less sail area to the wind). If you were to pull the boom across and just throw it across, you'll get a 'snap' when it hits the new side. That will be quite hard to steer to and match the body weight to. I want a nice, smooth gybe the whole way through. So what I do is, as the wind catches the boom on the new gybe, hold the boom for a brief moment and slowly ease the main out to the shroud – this will get rid of the snap effect.

Note the extra line hanging off the centre of the boom next to the mainsheet: this is the boom strap, which Dave grabs to force the boom over early during the gybe

GYBING IN LIGHT AIRS

Gybing asymmetrics in light airs is one of those things that's not difficult to do, but it's difficult to do well. Gybing from one gybe to the other takes time for the disturbed wind to re-attach on the new side of the sails, and it requires deft movement to keep the boat moving smoothly through the manoeuvre.

While a good general rule in asymmetric sailing is a 'flat boat at all times', here a bit of windward roll in the gybe will help keep the speed on through the manoeuvre and will give you the opportunity to pull the boat upright on the new gybe as you accelerate on to your new course.

In conditions where there's not sufficient wind to blow the kite past the forestay for the standard 'blow-through' gybe, now is the time to bring the 'pull-through' gybe into play. Because the wind is light and the boat is moving slowly, this is a fairly simple manoeuvre to execute.

Once you've gybed, sail high onto a reach to build the apparent wind on the new heading. As the boat accelerates and the power comes on again, you can then steer back to your normal heading. Look up and make sure that the mainsail battens have flicked through to the new gybe, which brings us on to our next section…

GYBING A FULLY-BATTENED MAINSAIL IN LIGHT AIRS

Fully battened mainsails put more power in the rig, which is great when you're going in a straight line. But fully-battened mainsails also make life more challenging through the manoeuvres, particularly through the gybe.

In light-to-medium conditions it can be difficult to convince all the battens to flick on to the new gybe when you are coming out of the manoeuvre. In fact, sometimes you can see people sailing along for hundreds of yards with the battens inverted

The exception that breaks the golden rule of 'Flat and Fast': this Swedish 49er applies heel and roll to their gybe in light winds, to help the battens flick over and to be able to accelerate the boat out of the gybe with crew weight; any windier than a Force 2, though, and all you want to do is gybe flat

International 14, for instance, it almost becomes part of the routine out of the gybe for the crew to reach forward, pull on an armful of cunningham until you can hear the batten pop and then release the cunningham again to get maximum power back into the mainsail. If you're doing a lot of gybing and the batten consistently refuses to pop through any gybe, it might even be worth leaving the cunningham on all the way down the run. What you lose in straight-line speed will be minimal compared with the time that you save from not faffing around trying to gybe that stubborn batten all the time.

In very light winds you will probably have to make sure that all the battens are gybed, because the force of the wind won't do any of the work for you. In these conditions, whoever in the boat is controlling the mainsail downwind has the responsibility of giving the boom a flick as the boat goes through the gybe. On many boats the best way to do this is to grab the boom directly, or by one of the mainsheet blocks hanging off the boom, and use that as a solid hand-hold to give the boom a vigorous shake just as you're gybing onto the new course.

In a single-handed boat like the Musto Skiff, this is really difficult because you're trying to gybe and set the kite through the manoeuvre and also make sure that the battens have popped. If you're struggling to do all these things at once, then make flicking the battens your top priority because it's much easier to do it smoothly, or at least do it during the course of the manoeuvre and then get the kite set later. It's much worse to come out of a gybe, get settled, and then look up and find that you've still got to shake those mainsail battens through. You'll then have to upset the balance and the trim of the boat to get that job done so you're really having to do everything twice. Give the battens your highest priority in light winds. Get them sorted and once the battens are through, then you can get on with all your other jobs.

because they haven't looked up and realised that the sail has refused to set properly by itself. There are times when it needs a helping hand. So, after a light wind gybe, make sure that you do look up and check the set of the sail.

In a boat with two people or less, this is the helm's job. In a boat where you have a full-time mainsheet hand then it's the mainsheet hand's job to check that these battens are behaving themselves. Quite often it's the top one or two battens that have failed to gybe. It might be that you can give the mainsail a couple of vigorous pumps to convince the battens to flick over, but make sure that you're staying within the rules when you do this. You don't want to be given a penalty by an umpire for looking like you're pumping the sail beyond the bounds of the dreaded Rule 42.

If a couple of vigorous pumps doesn't have the desired effect, then try tensioning the vang and even the cunningham. With the big square-headed mainsails that are in vogue with the really high-performance asymmetrics these days, such as the 18-foot Skiff and the International 14, the battens can be particularly stubborn. Gybing the

So far you've equipped yourself with the basic moves for getting you safely around a course. Now let's look at some of the more advanced moves and add a few more weapons to your armoury. One of the most daring moves is the gybe-set. Let's start there.

GYBE-SET

On most championship courses, the course is set for port roundings at the windward mark. The easiest and most straight forward hoist is a straight set on starboard gybe. But the ability to gybe set is an important addition to your tactical armoury. On a typical port-rounding course this sees you bearing away from close-hauled starboard tack onto starboard gybe, hoisting the gennaker, gybing onto port and filling the kite all in one smooth manoeuvre. You're sailing the boat through a tight arc of about 180 degrees, perhaps more.

Sound tricky? Well, it's not a beginner's move, but a great one to be able to use during a race. If you're rounding mid-fleet with lots of boats around you, most boats will be doing a straight set on starboard gybe, so the gybe-set has the potential to get you out into clear air very quickly.

PRACTISE FIRST

This is certainly not one to try first time out racing, and it's not one to try in strong winds. You want to practise this manoeuvre in light-to-medium airs.

The first thing to do is to get comfortable sailing from upwind, bearing away through a smooth arc and gybing the boat onto a port gybe. It's best to practise this first without hoisting the gennaker. Only bring the gennaker into play when you've got this manoeuvre down smoothly without it. Apart

from in very light winds, you want to keep the boat upright all the way through the manoeuvre.

Then, when you're comfortable doing it without the gennaker, try bringing the hoist into the process too. Initially, make sure you complete the full gybe and only start hoisting the gennaker when the boat is fully settled on port gybe.

At this point, it's the helm's responsibility to keep the boat upright while the crew stands up or does whatever is required to get in position to hoist the gennaker. On boats with the chute mouth located on the left-hand side of the foredeck, to one side of the jib, the hoist actually tends to be incredibly easy because the kite is unimpeded by the jib so it tends to be quite an easy few pulls getting the kite to the top of the mast.

However, it becomes even easier if the helmsman keeps the boat well borne away on a broad reach, possibly even a run. Applying a small amount of windward heel, say five degrees, means the kite is less likely to get tangled up with spreaders and rigging, creating a smoother passage up to the top of the mast.

One risk of hoisting the gennaker from this side of the boat, especially if you're not borne away on a dead run, is for the spinnaker to get stuck in the foretriangle, the space between the forestay and the mast. A great tip for helping avoid this is to have

This 49er just about gets away with the gybe, but when you are practising, build it up step by step

the jib sheeted on hard. Now, you only sheet the jib on hard when you've safely completed the whole gybing manoeuvre and you're travelling downwind, upright and in control. At that point if you pull the jib on hard, it will have no effect on the steering or stability of the boat. But what it will do is create a hard wall that will prevent the gennaker from getting stuck, giving the kite no choice but to blow out in front of the forestay. At this point the crew can snap on the gennaker sheet and get the kite filling nicely on port gybe. When the boat is up and running the crew can also ease the jib back to its normal downwind position.

SPEEDING IT UP

So that was the basic gybe-set. As you get more confident with the manoeuvre, you can speed up all the different phases of the process. The ultimate gybe-set is one where you start hoisting the gennaker, even as the boat is bearing away ready to gybe. The head of the kite hits the top of the mast, just as the boat is completing its gybe. The crew is already snapping on the new kite sheet whilst simultaneously hooking on to the port trapeze ring (if it is a trapeze dinghy) and pushing out off the side of the boat in unison with the helmsman as they catch the gennaker – just at the moment that the sail is filling and powering up.

This is an incredibly powerful manoeuvre and can accelerate the boat very quickly up to full speed on port gybe, enabling you to roll any other boats that have completed their gybe-set less effectively, as well as putting good distance between you and the boats that continued on starboard gybe on a straight set. However, you do need to be ready to apply full righting moment to the new windward side of the boat as you exit out of the gybe – if you're going to be able to control the power of the gennaker as it snaps into action. When you get this right, the acceleration is incredible, and it's one of the most rewarding manoeuvres you can do in an asymmetric boat.

As you bear away the crew moves inboard

And starts hoisting the kite

And continues hoisting

Rolling into a gybe when the kite is fully up

Once gybed, the crew pulls the spinnaker sheet

So the spinnaker fills on the new gybe

GYBE-DROP

If you can, start the gybe-drop nice and early in time for a clean mark rounding…

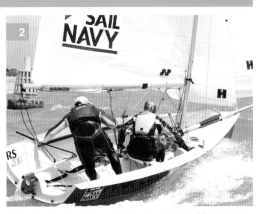

Dave pulls the boom to the centreline; Mari straps the kite in hard

Dave pulls the boom across, with minimal change in direction

With the boat slowing down, Dave eases the boom out to the shroud, keeping the boat flat

Mari get into position and stands up so she has a longer pull for arm-over-arm dropping

Mari retrieves the gennaker into the chute while Dave has steered in a wide arc, rounding up close to the buoy

The gybe-drop involves gybing and immediately dropping the gennaker all in one smooth manoeuvre. It's particularly useful for approaching a leeward mark to leeward of other boats and claiming inside mark-rounding rights.

As with all manoeuvres involving hoisting or dropping the gennaker, it's vital the helm provides a stable and upright platform so that the crew can get on with stowing the gennaker as quickly as possible without interruption or feeling they need to help balance the boat.

GYBE DROPPING INTO A CHUTE

In terms of boat handling, the gybe-drop requires more balance and timing than a straight drop. The key is to go into the gybe at full speed, just as you would on a normal gybe. The difference comes once you've gybed, at which point the helm needs to keep the boat borne away close to a dead run, as the crew will be aiming to get the kite down and in the chute as soon as the gybe is complete. If the crew keeps the old kite sheet tensioned as you go into the gybe, this will keep the three corners of the sail nicely separated and will encourage the kite to go into the chute untwisted, ready for a clean hoist next time.

GYBE DROPPING INTO A BAG

On a dinghy like a B14 or 18-foot Skiff, gybe dropping from starboard gybe onto port ensures you'll be correctly set up for a leeward hoist at the next windward mark. So the gybe-drop is even more important for boats with gennaker bags. The straight drop into a bag is not a particularly easy manoeuvre, not compared with the simplicity of dropping into a chute. You might as well get used to the gybe-drop as one of your standard manoeuvres.

The approach and initial phase is the same as a standard gybe. But, again, once the gybe is complete, don't steer up but keep the boat tracking downwind on, or near, a dead run. This takes all the apparent wind out of the kite and makes it easier for the crew to bag.

And again, like the gybe-drop into a chute, if the crew keeps the kite sheeted in with the old gennaker sheet as they gybe, the kite is sitting there next to you, ready to grab and easy to reach for the take-down. Release the tack line first, getting the tack of the sail safely back on to the foredeck where it can't fall in the water, then release the halyard and stuff the sail into the bag as gravity gives you a helping hand. Once the kite is stowed, make sure the bowsprit is retracted back into the boat.

BEAM REACHING

Beam reaching is one of the first things that we learn to do in sailing, because it's one of the easiest things to do. In fast, lightweight skiffs, the opposite is true. Because they are so quick to accelerate and build on their own apparent wind, they become too efficient for their own good.

In moderate-to-strong winds, sailing directly on a beam reach from one mark to another becomes impossible. As the boat accelerates and the apparent wind builds, the power rapidly increases and exceeds the righting moment available. Either you capsize, or you change direction. You need to sail below the rhumb line (low mode), or above it (high mode), or a combination of the two. So, to stay upright and in control, you actually end up sailing a zig-zag course to the mark. In skiff world, the no-go zone is known as the 'death zone'.

Spend as little time as possible in the 'death zone'

At any point during the reach, everyone on board needs to understand whether the helm is sailing in a high mode or a low mode. Keep a constant look out over your windward shoulder for the next gust. If you're in high mode, get ready to luff up and ease main and jib together. Make sure the boat is slightly heeled to windward before the gust hits. Once you're in the gust, get settled on the new course and look out for the next change in wind speed, whether it's a gust or a lull.

If you're sailing in low mode, again you need to keep a weather eye out for the next gust, but this time as the gust hits you bear away and ease sails to keep the boat on its feet. Once you have accelerated with the gust, head up as close to the direction of the mark as the power will allow. Sheet the sails to keep the boat flat. Generally, a reach requires massive amounts of mainsheet to move in and out, and boats where the crew plays the mainsheet are at a massive advantage because they have two arms to devote to the task. Helms who play the mainsheet are more restricted in how much sheet they can move, so steering becomes even more critical.

Whether you are in high or low mode, it is all about sailing as close to the death zone as you can without becoming overpowered. Sailing down a beam reach is one of the most challenging things you can do in a high-performance boat. But it's great fun when you master the technique.

BOAT SET-UP

Sailing down a beam reach is mostly about courage and good technique, but good boat set-up will also make things easier. Do anything you can to depower the boat. This can include any or all of the following:

- Pull up daggerboard / centreboard
- Maximum cunningham
- Maximum outhaul
- Minimum vang
- Jib out on widest traveller car setting (if you have a track for a self-tacking jib for example)
- Mainsail traveller fully to leeward

Remember, once you're already on the tight reach, it will be much harder or impossible to make these adjustments, so try to anticipate and alter the boat set-up before you get to that point.

Beam reaching in a boat like a Devoti D-One is simple enough, but requires more respect in a high-powered skiff

TIGHT REACHING

Recent years have seen sailing become more and more focused on windward / leeward courses, with sailors becoming very specialised in the techniques of beating and running. This is particularly true in asymmetric racing where the only kind of courses are windward / leeward.

There are some classes like the International 14 which have always included reaches in their championship courses and continue to do so today. Also, many of us race around the cans in club racing in handicap fleets, and the ability to reach with an asymmetric sail becomes a vital skill.

Even if you only ever race on windward / leeward courses, I strongly advise you to practise your tight reaching skills. You only need to overstand a downwind layline by a small amount, or to be on your layline when suddenly the wind increases by 5 knots, when you now find yourself well below the layline.

Pushing it high in an 18-footer

DE-TUNE THE BOAT

Early on in this book, we established that, in planing conditions, the higher you point the more apparent wind you create, and the deeper and faster you end up sailing. All these things are great when you are trying to make maximum ground downwind. But

all these wonderful efficiencies are now working against you as you try to make maximum ground to windward with the kite up.

You will actually make better ground to windward if you can slow the boat down and get rid of some of that apparent wind. Here are some things you can do to help slow the boat and gain height:

- Pull on cunningham
- Ease vang
- Ease jibsheet
- Ease mainsheet
- Daggerboard / centreboard up
- Let the boat heel over to leeward
- Ease the kite to maximum curl before it flogs, or
- Oversheet the kite!

An International 14 pushing for height, the crew curling the gennaker as much as possible

Oversheeting the kite feels like absolutely the wrong thing to do, but I've tried it a few times in different classes and it works surprisingly well for slowing the boat down and gaining height to windward. Another extreme option I learnt when crewing for Will Henderson (multiple champion in the International 14) was to jump up and down on the gunwale whilst we were twin-trapezing in the International 14. Will's theory was that if smooth is fast, then rough is slow! If it reduces the efficiency of the boat, then it might well work. We didn't do it often enough to prove it one way or the other. But the overriding message here is to think of ways that you can make the boat less efficient! The more you can reduce the apparent wind, the higher you will point.

Nothing like the pressure of a rocky shore to hone your tight reaching skills!

Ben Saxton: Goosewinging

This is a radical move where you 'goosewing' the gennaker on the opposite side to the boom and run dead downwind, with the flow going from leech to luff. Here's Ben Saxton's take on this unusual manoeuvre.

It's banned in the RS200 but it's legal to goosewing in some boats, and it can work quite well in light-to-medium winds. Technique-wise, it's pretty straightforward; a bit of windward heel helps to swing the gennaker out to windward and project it away from the mainsail. It doesn't work in really light winds when you need to be sailing big angles to build the apparent wind, but between 7 to 12 knots of true wind and the goosewing option starts to get interesting.

It's often not that quicker in VMG terms but it is a very useful tactical option. We used it at the 2020 Bacardi Cup in Miami, which we went on to win. There was one race where we had a bad start and rounded the windward mark in about 15th. We went straight into goosewing mode while most of the fleet were fighting each other for the high lane. So there's that period where most of the fleet are sailing nowhere close to VMG as they're battling for position, sailing big arcs. Anyway, it went well, because we were leading by the leeward mark. We did it again that day because the breeze was very stable and there weren't many tactical opportunities, so we went into goosewing out of another windward mark and found it to be marginally quicker, so we just stuck with it. The other time to consider it is approaching the leeward mark where you're on port gybe and want to gain starboard advantage, so you leave the kite where it is but flip the boom across the centreline and now you've got starboard rights.

EXPERT ADVICE

Stevie Morrison: Great boat handling makes for great tactics

Stevie Morrison and Ben Rhodes won the 49er Worlds in Cascais 2007. One race in particular was really whacky, with wildly shifting and gusting breeze, but somehow Stevie and Ben got their heads around it. Great boat handling enabled them to make some great tactical calls. Stevie looks back on a crazy race that went almost perfectly.

The race course was right under the shore at Cascais so very shifty, gusting between 6 and 20 knots. I remember it being a moment on the first beat where the wind had shifted left, then really hard right, and I just said to Ben: 'Look, we're just going to point at the mark and see which way the wind takes us for a moment.' We were pretty much aimed straight at the windward mark with sails in the middle of the boat and lying in about 10th place and like 'Oh blimey, this is going to be quite a race.'

A couple of good little shifts later, and we were 3rd or 4th at the windward mark. I always remember down the first run we found a gust there when we needed it, and obviously there's an element of luck to that. Ben and I managed to just hit that gust and did about seven or eight gybes down the first run. We went straight down the middle of the run, kind of bouncing off the other boats that were ahead of us, and by the leeward mark we were probably a good 200 metres ahead of the second-placed boat, which was obviously pretty nice.

It was a three-lap race and we just seemed to hit pretty much every shift. What I remember most fondly about the whole thing – and this will probably come back to bite me in the bum one day – was as we were going down the third run, we took a little gust and we went past Nathan Outteridge [multiple World Champion from Australia]. We lapped Nathan as he was coming down to the finish, I think he still finished 10th or 11th in the race and still ended up with a bronze medal at that Worlds.

Looking back on it, I think our philosophy of tacking when the jib flapped worked well for us. And downwind in a 49er you can get a gust and if you use it right you can stay with it for pretty much the whole leg. I think where we did a good job in that race – and what's pretty key in a fast asymmetric boat – is having that ability to make sure you don't sail yourself off a gust and into a lull.

Having the boat-handling skills to put in six or seven gybes in a two or three minute run, that's the main lesson. It's really important to have the boat handling to keep clinging on to that gust. So as soon as we even had a hint of the wind going at all light, we were gybing straight back across the gust. You've got to have the boat-handling skills to be able to throw in as many gybes as you need if it's appropriate.

Stevie Morrison and Ben Rhodes on their way to winning the 49er Worlds in Cascais

PART 2
STRONG WINDS

SURVIVAL SAILING

Once you've got the basic manoeuvres squared away in light-to-medium winds, you can then start looking at wrestling the boat around the race course in strong winds. Sailing high-performance boats in big wind and waves is not for the faint-hearted, but then you're not one of the faint-hearted, are you! Let's kick off with one of the biggest manoeuvres of all, bearing away in a big breeze...

EXTREME BEAR-AWAY

Bearing away from a beat onto a downwind course can be very challenging in high-speed skiffs. We've already mentioned the danger of the 'death zone' in the previous chapter. Well, this manoeuvre takes you right through that zone, so the key is to minimise the time you spend there. In a 49er – one of the most difficult skiffs to bear away in a breeze – the key is to go from upwind to downwind in the shortest possible time.

As you approach the windward mark, release the vang to its downwind position, get the jib out of the cleat ready to ease. Just before the crucial moment, get to the back of the boat, with the windward wing down flat to the water, one foot in the footloop for the helm, ease the jib and pull her away. But don't even think about bearing away unless the boat is flat or slightly heeled to windward. If it's not, bail out, get yourself ready again, and start from the

The nose buries as Chris Draper and Simon Hiscocks turn their 49er downwind

beginning. Even if you're sailing well above the windward mark by this stage, it's better to go the extra distance rather than lose patience and fall in.

As for who takes the mainsheet at this stage, it's whatever you feel more comfortable with. As the helm I like to take the mainsheet for the manoeuvre, but it's personal preference.

One universal rule: be committed to it. It's about clear communication, and you might even count down into the bear-away. Waves are an issue, so better to sail on a reach to sail clear of other boats, before you do the manoeuvre. The bear-away and the kite hoist are totally separate manoeuvres, so treat them as such. Wait for your moment before you hoist the kite.

Commit to the bear-away, and tell the boat who's boss

EXTREME CONDITIONS

STRAIGHT-LINE SURVIVAL WITH THE GENNAKER

Getting downwind in big breeze with the gennaker can be scary if you let the boat run away with itself. In most boats, you're trying to drive them as hard as possible all the time, but if you do that in high-performance skiffs there's a danger of nose-diving and pitchpoling, sending you flying over the front of the boat – or worse, into the rig.

If you're sailing significantly faster than the waves, then you're at risk of nose-diving. At this point you should treat the gennaker sheet as the throttle on the engine. The closer you set the gennaker to optimum trim, the faster you will go and the more risk you are taking. So you have two options: oversheet the kite or flap it.

If you are consistently too fast, then oversheet the kite as much as you need to feel comfortable. The more you oversheet, the slower the boat will go.

If you can cope with max speed most of the time, and it's just the occasional wave where you think you could

come to grief, then flap the gennaker until you've overtaken the wave and the moment of danger has passed. Then oversheet the kite and get going again.

Keep the mainsheet on fairly tight. With a masthead-rigged asymmetric, the mainsail leech will help support the mast and work as a form of backstay. But even if you're sailing a boat that doesn't have a full-hoist gennaker, keeping the mainsail sheeted in will stop the top of the leech leaning over the front of the boat. This will help reduce the tendency of the rig to drive the bow down, and the boat will feel safer and easier to steer.

If you're worried about nose-diving, curl the gennaker or oversheet it

PART 2
66

SURVIVAL SAILING WITHOUT THE GENNAKER

In a lot of asymmetrics it's easier getting downwind in survival conditions with the kite hoisted. The sail provides extra lift to the bow, and if you do nose-dive, the water has a much clearer run through the boat and the empty chute. With the kite in the chute, any water rushing over the bow has a much harder time moving through the cockpit, the resistance builds up and ... over you go.

That said, in extreme conditions, getting the kite up in the first place is easier said than done. And, in any case, you need to know how to get downwind without the kite for getting position for the pre-start

and other situations outside of racing. You need to know how to get safely downwind without the gennaker.

OVERSHEET THE MAINSAIL

As we mentioned in the previous section, the problems arise when the boat is travelling faster than the waves, setting up a perfect scenario for a nose-dive. So the answer is to try to match wave speed. How to achieve this? By oversheeting the mainsail. If you are running downwind and you have the boom out to the shroud, you are presenting

Getting downwind without the kite can be even more challenging...

maximum sail area to the wind. By pulling in the mainsail, then, you are effectively reducing sail area. In other words, oversheeting is a very crude form of reefing. Crude, but effective.

The mainsail is well sheeted in, but with the crew dropping the kite, the mainsail will load up quickly. This team is just about getting away with it

STEER ACROSS THE WAVES

The other thing you can do is to always steer across the waves, never directly into the back of them. Mimic a Laser / ILCA dinghy, which alternates between broad reaching across the wave, and then bearing away until it's running by the lee. This will mean the wind is blowing from leech to luff of the mainsail, and you are not far from a gybe. So this method is not without its risks, but it might be preferable to constantly spearing into the back of the next wave and pitchpoling.

SURVIVAL GYBE

In survival conditions, where just getting around the race course is a victory in itself, then it's worth knowing a gybing technique which certainly has served me well in 49ers and International 14s and probably applies to most high-performance asymmetrics.

In really strong winds, any gybe where you stay upright is a good gybe!

The modification from a standard gybe is very simple. The entry is exactly the same – it's all about keeping maximum speed on as long as possible into the manoeuvre. Remember, the faster you are, the safer you'll be.

For the crew, everything else is the same as a standard gybe except that, as you go into the gybe, and the crew runs through the boat, you just keep on hauling on the old kite sheet and keep it pinned in.

When you come out of the gybe onto the new side, you're now looking at the strange sight of a tightly strapped gennaker with the wind blowing across it from back to front, i.e. from leech to luff. It might look weird, but you'll find you can actually steer out of the gybe onto your new heading in a very controlled manner.

The nice thing about it is that while the boat went through the gybe quickly (which is the safest way), it's now travelling quite slowly, which means the boat isn't leaping from wave top to wave top as quickly as it might be if the gennaker was set for maximum speed. This gives you ample opportunity to get hooked up onto the trapeze and into your foot loops.

Once you've settled and you're ready to hit hyperspace, the crew releases the old kite sheet, the gennaker blows past the forestay, and you can set the kite again for maximum speed. Or at least as much speed the conditions will allow.

WARNING TO HIKING SAILORS

I asked Geoff Carveth and Dave Hivey how they thought this technique would apply to slower asymmetrics like RS200s and RS400s, and they didn't reckon it would work. First, you don't have the same righting moment available, as there are no trapezes; and second, the kite is relatively small compared with the mainsail. Both experts reckon you want to get the kite gybed and set as soon as possible out of the manoeuvre, to get the boat up to speed and get the pressure off the mainsail. They thought that trying this 'safety gybe' could result in a broach. But for trapeze skiffs with masthead gennakers, I can't recommend the technique highly enough.

The RS200 has a big mainsail and a small gennaker, so get the kite filling and powered up as fast as possible out of the gybe

---

EXPERT ADVICE

Trevor Bayliss: Safety gybing – verbal guarantee

Gybing technique is one of the toughest and most critical elements of skiff sailing, but Trevor Baylis (World Champion in 14s, 18s and 505s) has some ideas that will help make heavy air gybing a whole lot safer...

> *One thing I will say to my helmsman in fresh conditions is: 'I will be out on the wire on the other side. Don't stop the turn.' A lot of helms S-turn out of the exit, but this is where you can start to get in trouble. It's much more comforting for the helm to know he can keep on steering high out of the gybe, knowing that you're going to be on the wire for him. Even if you can't guarantee that you'll have the kite set, at least you'll be on the wire.*
>
> *There have been some occasions where it's been so windy that I've not even bothered picking up the new kite sheet. At the International 14 World Championships in Bermuda, we had the sea wall at the leeward mark and waves coming back at you, and we knew that if we capsized there would be a high chance of breaking the mast. So we just had to be really conservative. We just crossed the boat, we'd both come out with the kite flogging, and get our feet in the foot loops. The boat wouldn't be going that fast, but we'd be pretty safe. Zach would get settled, and then I'd reach forward and pick up the sheet, set the kite and get going again. If you haven't tried it, you'll be amazed just how stable the boat is even with the kite flogging like that.*

In high winds, move through the boat as fast as possible, and worry about setting the kite afterwards

TACKING

Part of what makes lightweight skiffs so attractive – their light weight, that is – is also what makes them a real beast when trying to tack them in strong winds. With a lack of hull weight, the boat stops easily, particularly with all the wind resistance and drag of a big, fully-battened rig as it starts to flog. The boat slows down easily and, if you hang around too long during the tack, it can stop altogether or start going backwards. I've even seen a B14 capsizing backwards, bow over stern!

Halfway through a windy tack, the boat is at risk of becoming very unstable and unpredictable. Just as a fast gybe is a safe gybe, the same is true of tacking a high-performance skiff. Coming into a tack, aim to sail the boat totally flat, steering slowly into it. The more controlled your entry, the better your exit. If you go through too heeled, it swings through too quickly on the new tack, or refuses to tack at all.

Getting blown in to leeward on the new tack is the most common problem, so you might have to watch the crew and see how quickly they react. Be ready to let the jib go if they are slow getting on to the new side. The helm's priority is steering and, as long as he holds it head-to-wind long enough to give the crew time to move to the new side, you should be fine.

If you have a self-tacking jib, ease the sheet 15cm (six inches) before the tack, this will give the helm a wider steering groove out of the tack. Oversteering out of the tack with a tightly pinned jib is sure to capsize you.

In a single-handed skiff like the Musto Skiff, you have no jib to help pull the bow away from the breeze. The important thing here is to maintain enough speed to drive the boat all the way through the turn and out on to a close reach. Don't even think about pointing up on the new heading until you've got the boat moving on a close reach. As always, the key to getting through the tack is a flat and fast boat, and when you don't have a jib this becomes even more important.

In waves, look for a flat spot in which to complete your tack. Be clear with your commands (in a two-man boat), and when you go for it you've got to be committed to it.

Get the skiff through the eye of the wind before it loses too much speed and stalls

AVOIDING DISASTER

All sailboat racing is about minimising your mistakes. The sailor that makes the least mistakes is the winner. It might seem a negative way of looking at things, but it's still quite a useful one. And it's particularly relevant to high-performance boats that are difficult to sail. In strong winds, if you can avoid all the big mistakes – e.g. capsizing, collisions, pitchpoles and so on – then you'll probably do very well.

In this chapter we look at some of the biggest mistakes, and how to avoid them.

MAKE A PLAN

First, let's talk about a general philosophy; about knowing what you're about, and what your aims are. In team boats, this is particularly important. Everyone on board needs to know what the game plan is before you start, in fact before you even go afloat. As former 49er World medallist, 505 World Champion and America's Cup veteran Morgan Larson puts it. *"Even a bad plan is better than no plan. Of course, if I get a bad start – which I often do – then you need a Plan B!"* Not that Morgan does get many bad starts, but I hope you understand the point. A boat, and a team, that knows where it's going, is much more likely to get there!

Discuss your plan before the race: Olympic 49er Champions Iker Martinez and Xabi Fernandez, deep in thought

PREPARE FOR THE UNEXPECTED

This follows on from the previous point and is one of the most overlooked aspects of sailing.

When you go out and practise, it's too easy just to go through the standard manoeuvres such as tacking and gybing, and maybe some mark roundings. But what about practising for when things go wrong, such as 720° penalty turns and capsizes? The best way to practise is to put yourself in these pressure situations and see how you respond.

The other classic thing in many asymmetric and one-design classes, which do nearly all their racing on windward / leeward courses, is not to bother how to two-sail reach because you never have to do it. Then, one day, when the wind shifts and the course gets all skewed, suddenly you have to start two-sail reaching, which is the toughest point of sailing in a boat like the 49er. Times like these really reveal which teams have been putting in the practice for those rare eventualities – and which ones haven't.

Another common mistake is only to practise bear-aways on starboard tack, because that is what you normally do on a port-rounding course. Bearing away in a 49er is a pretty tough exercise in strong winds. It's easy to pitchpole or capsize if

Roger Gilbert and Ben McGrane on an 'untypical' port bear-away in the International 14

you get your timing wrong, so teams practise their bearing away until it works like clockwork. However, try bearing away on the other gybe – and it feels totally alien. This is what Chris Draper and Simon Hiscocks discovered in the build-up to the Athens Olympics, when they struggled to bear the boat away on port during an important race in big winds.

So, after getting home from the regatta, Chris and Simon went out into Weymouth Bay and put a hard training session in, purely to conquer this one manoeuvre. It didn't take them long before the

port bear-away felt like second nature, and it was another weapon in their armoury. Whether they've had to use it in anger since then, I don't know. Probably not very often, if at all, but the strangest things often happen at the most crucial of moments.

And I do remember seeing one race at Athens 2004 where the wind shifted massively, putting all the 49ers on to a very tight gennaker reach. Unfamiliar territory for all but the most prepared of teams, who made hay while others made a hash of getting through the leeward gate in good shape.

TRAWLING THE KITE

Trawling the kite is a horrible feeling. It can happen when you're hoisting the gennaker but then part of the sail flops into the water and then the next moment the whole thing is in the sea, trawling like a fisherman's net.

The boat slows to a near standstill, and puts massive strain on the sail, and the mast. If the sail has completely fallen in the water, you will need to turn up into the wind and stop the boat completely. Then the crew will need to reach over the side and man-handle the soggy sail back on to the deck, and ideally stow it in the bag or chute before you get going again.

Sometimes, if just one corner of the sail falls into the water, there's a chance of saving yourself from trawling humiliation by powering through the rest of the hoist as quickly as possible.

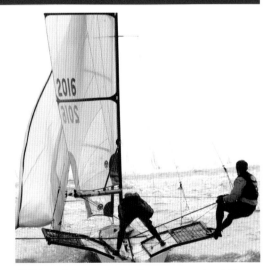

At this point of the hoist, the crew must pull like mad to avoid the dreaded 'trawl'

EXPERT ADVICE

Steve Irish: Avoiding the trawl

For another perspective, I asked former RS800 Champion Steve Irish about the dreaded trawl, and how to avoid it.

> *Leeward heel is the main reason why the trawl happens. So, from a helming point of view, you've got to make sure you do bear away far enough that you've got the boat slightly over on top – and that just gives the kite that little bit of air before it has a chance to hit the water. Make sure that the crew doesn't rush into the hoist too much. They've got to be ready. At the start of the hoist they've got to be fully solid in the bottom of the boat and once they start the hoist that it's one continuous movement and doesn't get stopped at any point. A lot of trawls tend to happen when the crew started the hoist because they're desperate to get it going – and then find they have to re-position or stop. Then the kite just droops slightly, catches the water and suddenly the job becomes twice as hard.*
>
> *On the sea, the helm should be looking for the right wave so, when you call the hoist, you should be happy that you can sit on the face of one wave for the whole of the hoist. You're also looking then just to keep a real constant heel angle, so the crew's balance isn't being knocked at all. If you can do that, then you should be perfectly alright. If we did start to get a trawl in the RS800, I'd shout at my crew to 'pull it hard,' and he was usually big enough that he could normally rip it back out of the water without it developing into a full-on trawl.*

TWIST IN THE KITE

If the gennaker goes up with an 'hourglass' twist, then you need to pay attention to how the kite is stowed during the drops. Keeping some tension in the gennaker sheet will make it much harder for the kite to twist on the way into the bag or chute. It's when you let the kite flog before you drop it that the problems occur. So keeping sheet tension on as late as possible is the key to twist prevention.

But what if the kite has twisted? Try the following remedies, in this order:

1. Oversheet the gennaker, pulling it all the way in, then releasing, and pulling all the way in again. Sometimes the kite can untwist itself just by doing this, but if the kite is still twisted…

2. Ease the halyard half a metre, then try oversheeting again. As soon as the kite untwists, re-hoist the halyard. However, if the kite is still twisted…

3. Gybe, keeping as much tension on the old sheet as possible. The act of gybing will shake out all but the very worst of twists

If none of these remedies works, then this really is a major twist, and you may well need to drop the gennaker to the deck and manually untwist the sail. But this doesn't happen very often.

Trying to untwist the kite on a Rebel Skiff

KEEP A LOOKOUT DOWNWIND

With most modern gennakers setting quite close to the water, this can create a large blind spot to leeward when you're travelling downwind. If your class doesn't permit windows in the gennaker, you have to find other ways of keeping an eye out downwind.

When both of you are on a trapeze in an International 14 or a 49er for example, it's very difficult to know what's going on ahead and to leeward of you. One thing you can do is to sail the boat very flat, or almost heel to windward, provided that you're very low on the trapeze. But, in light-to-medium conditions, this isn't always practical. So it could be that either the helm or the crew needs to move to leeward occasionally, just to get a sense of where the boats are on the upwind leg, so that you know if there's a possibility that you might be on a collision course and you can do something about it.

You might also hope that the boat coming upwind will give adequate notice by hailing to you and making you aware of the fact that they are there. Self preservation might suggest that that would be the sensible thing to do but, in my experience, this does not always happen, whether it's because the other sailors feel intimidated by the sight of a fast asymmetric coming towards them, or they don't feel the need to tell you. There's certainly no onus under the racing rules for them to tell you, so get in the habit of looking to leeward every minute or so.

The gennaker can create a blind spot for helm and crew

COLLISION COURSE? OVERSHEET THE KITE

If you're sailing downwind on port gybe in a good puff, and you find yourself on a collision course with a boat on starboard, what do you do? Most people gybe, which is fine if that's what you want to do anyway. But what if you're already on the favoured gybe and want to continue on port?

Sheet in the gennaker as hard as possible and the boat will slow down significantly. Let the starboard boat pass safely in front, then release the sheet until the gennaker is setting nicely again. Yes, you've given away ground, but you've maintained control over your tactics rather than being dictated to by the other boat.

The helmsman has stepped in and oversheeted the kite to slow the boat down rather than gybe

EXPERT ADVICE

Dave Hivey: Practising taking penalties

RS200 Champion Dave Hivey practises his penalties. Most good sailors do:

It's a good boat handling exercise anyway. The general rule is tack first when you're sailing upwind and gybe first when you're heading downwind. When you're doing the turn – whether it's a 360° or 720° turn – make sure that you keep the mainsheet playing the whole way through the gybe. You've got to sheet really hard, really fast on the mainsheet as you're spinning the boat into the wind to get that drive from the leech of the mainsail. That will get you safely through the tack, at which point you ease the jib and mainsail as you bear away straight into a gybe.

Equally important is paying attention to the heel of the boat. Whenever you're turning into the wind, the boat should be heeled away from you, and whenever you're turning away from the wind, the boat's got to be heeled over on top of you. You've got to make sure that you keep to that rule all the way through and then the boat will keep spinning through the turn. If you ever let the heel go the wrong way at any point, the boat is in danger of stalling.

David Hivey practises 360° turns in case he gets a penalty during racing

Just like any dinghy, a modern asymmetric dinghy is quite capable of capsizing, and some of the high-performance ones are more prone to capsizing than most.

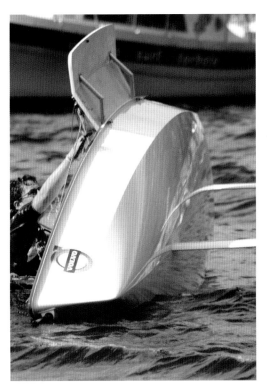

Even the author takes the occasional swim!

You can see this when you launch a boat like a 49er or International 14. You can't just hold onto it at the bow by the forestay and expect the boat to stay upright by itself like you'd expect a Fireball or a Laser to stay upright, for example.

High-performance skiffs naturally want to fall over because they're narrow on the waterline and they have tall rigs.

You're dealing with something that's inherently unstable, although, as we've said before, it's a little bit like a bicycle. The more speed you have going forwards, the more stable the boat tends to become.

That's the thing to bear in mind whenever you're sailing the boat – if you can keep the speed on through a manoeuvre, you have a much better chance of staying upright.

WHY CAPSIZES HAPPEN

GYBING

One of the most common places for a capsize, like any other dinghy, is in a gybe, particularly when it's windy. We've already said that it's very important to keep an asymmetric dinghy upright at all times. Rolling the boat to windward in a gybe is not a good thing, unless the wind is really light and you're looking for some roll to help flick the battens through the gybe.

If you do capsize, it could be for a number of reasons. Beginners tend to apply too much rudder to the turn, turning far too quickly, in too tight an arc. This creates a momentum in the top of the rig which is hard to fight. After you've capsized a few times doing this, you'll soon understand what I mean, and you'll start using the rudder much less than perhaps you did initially. If you do capsize to windward after a gybe, the chances are that you'll end up in the water next to the boom.

Crossing the boat too late is a common cause of capsizing

LEEWARD MARK

Another danger spot on the race course is at the leeward mark. If you round up quickly and with the boat slightly heeled to leeward, it can be very difficult coping with the sudden increase in power. Getting thrown in to leeward is the risk here.

SUDDEN GUSTS OR LULLS

Dealing with sudden gusts and lulls, or big wind shifts, is a challenge. If you sail into a lull or a header, the boat can come on top of you and capsize to windward. Unhooking from the trapeze can unweight the boat and, if you're lucky, the wind will blow the boat upright again. Of course, you've now got to haul yourself back into the boat, but this is preferable to a total capsize.

PITCHPOLE OR NOSE-DIVE

In strong winds there's the risk of the pitchpole, capsizing over the bow. We've already looked at that, flapping the kite and other slowing down techniques (p65). But every so often you'll get it wrong, and a capsize will unfortunately be the inevitable outcome.

Almost any boat is capable of capsizing sideways. High-performance skiffs offer the additional fun of capsizing forwards, a.k.a. the nose-dive! Sometimes you can survive it, after you've witnessed 'green water' washing over the bow and through the cockpit. But sometimes you have to accept that the nose-dive is just one of those things that comes as part and parcel of high-performance sailing.

Going...

Going...

Gone!

OK, SO YOU'VE CAPSIZED, WHAT NOW?

SAFETY FIRST

Much of what you do next depends on the particular characteristics of your boat. First thing to do is to make sure that you and your crew are clear of any ropes and, particularly, that any trapeze hooks are not tangled up with anything. If they are, then getting untangled is the top priority. If swimming clear isn't possible, then be ready to cut the tangled line or the trapeze harness if necessary. For this reason, I strongly advise you to keep a knife on board (see p19). On the 18ft Skiff class, having a knife attached to the aft port trapeze rack is a class rule so that, in the event of a capsize and one of the crew being caught in the water, anyone will know where to find a knife, even one of the rescue boats. This is a great example to follow and all high-performance sailors should do it.

AVOID THE 'TURTLE'

When you're sure that everyone is clear of the rigging and people are free to move in the water, your next priority should be to prevent the boat from going turtle, i.e. from turning upside down. This might involve one or both of you going straight round to the daggerboard / centreboard and catching the boat before it inverts completely.

PART 2

77

First check everyone's OK

Close to turtle – i.e. upside down – which will make getting the boat upright even longer and more arduous

BAG THE KITE

If you're confident that your kind of boat is not so prone to inverting and you think you've got time to get the gennaker back into its chute while the boat is still on its side, then this is the next priority. If the kite was fully hoisted and cleated when you capsized, be careful about releasing the halyard from the cleat straight away. Whilst the luff of the kite is pulled tight, it can't wrap around the forestay, the jib or anything else. Once you release that cleat, the kite can create all kinds of havoc, potentially tying itself in knots around the forestay, especially in a boat like the Musto Skiff without even a jib to keep the kite from creating mayhem. Only when you have stabilised the boat to the point where you're sure that it's going to stay on its side, should you get the kite back into the chute.

If you find that you're struggling to get it back in, firstly check that the halyard hasn't re-cleated. If you have a jib, pull the jib in quite hard, so that there's a hard surface for the kite to bear against and this will minimise the danger of the kite wrapping itself around the forestay.

Having a newer kite with stiffer cloth tends to be less prone to wrapping itself around the jib or forestay. So, alongside the benefits of a newer sail being slightly faster and easier to get in and out of the chute and through racing manoeuvres, another good reason is your ability to retrieve the kite safely.

GETTING UPRIGHT

When you've got the chute back in, you can start thinking about bringing the boat upright. Some boats respond well to having lots of vang and cunningham pulled on to the mainsail, because this flattens it off and makes it more easy for the water to flow off the sail, making it much easier to pull the boat upright. Experiment with different tensions in these controls until you find what works best for your type of boat. You'll be surprised how much difference these sail controls can make.

When you're ready to pull the boat upright, make sure that the mainsheet is uncleated and (once the kite is stowed in the chute) that the jibsheet is also uncleated. It can pay to keep the jib loosely sheeted and then release the cleat at the last moment when you believe that the boat is actually coming upright, because a loose jib lying around in the water can wrap itself around the forestay. In the case of a fully battened jib, you can end up with broken battens, so keeping the jib tensioned for as long as possible will help minimise sail damage.

The next thing to decide is which way up the boat is going to come in relation to the wind. A lot of boats when they're in the water tend to rotate around until the mast is facing upwind. A 49er is one such boat, and this means that, as you manage to pull the mast tip out of the water, the wind will gradually catch underneath the underside of the sail until the wind lifts the sail up and flips it upright with some force. The most likely outcome is that the wind will flip it all the way over and capsize the boat to leeward. This gives you another capsize to recover from, so here's the technique for preventing the 'double capsize'.

Helm and crew work together on the daggerboard / centreboard until the mast and sails are lying flat on the water

Then the crew (being the heavier) stays on the board while the helm swims round to the cockpit

Crew pulls mast out of the water – with the mast pointing towards the wind

Once the wind gets under the sails the boat comes upright very quickly, so the crew moves fast to get on board while he can

The helm stabilises the boat sufficiently for the nimble crew to get on board, avoiding a follow-on capsize

But the crew is still in front of the mast and needs to get aft at the first opportunity: from there he can join his helm on the wing and help get the boat moving again

PREVENTING THE BOAT FROM FLIPPING

First you need to have helm and crew standing on the board. As the boat comes upright and as the mast tip shows signs of wanting to lift from the water, the lighter of the two of you should jump down into the water between the gap between the deck and the boom. The helmsman or whoever has gone into the water, clips onto the helm's trapeze ring which is lying in the water, grabs hold of the mainsheet without tensioning it, grabs hold of the tiller and waits for the crew to pull the mast out of the water. As the mast blows upright, the sailor attached to the trapeze wire needs to stay put, keeping your bottom sitting on what will now be the new windward rack. With the speed that the boat comes upright, it can be unnerving going through this process, but you'll find that the end result is surprisingly calm with the boat settling back in upright mode. Most of the time you will avoid the follow-on capsize to leeward because your weight has counteracted the force of the boat being blown over to leeward.

If, however, it's really windy and you do feel the boat going the other way, if you're quick enough, you can jump onto the trapeze and apply more righting moment to stop this happening. If the boat continues to capsize, then be ready to jump out the back of the boat beyond the mainsail. Fall from that height into the mainsail, and you may will put a sailor-shaped hole in it! Make sure you leap before you fall.

The boat comes upright, but that doesn't always mean you're home and dry...

Maximum effort now could save you having to endure a secondary capsize

THE ESKIMO ROLL

If it's really windy or the technique above doesn't work, then one of you needs to commit to the cause a little more. Whoever has been standing on the board to get the mast out of the water now needs to commit to the 'Eskimo roll'. As the boat comes upright, grab on to the board and stay with it. This means you're going underwater, but most likely not for long.

The Eskimo roll may sound unpleasant, but it's really not that bad. Your body resistance and your body weight helps slow down the rate of turn and reduces the likelihood of the boat doing a further capsize, so if the crew holds onto the daggerboard / centreboard until such time as the boat settles down in an upright position, you can push yourself out from underneath the boat and come up to one or other of the gunwales and work out which side of the boat you should get back into.

If it's windy, or you don't manage to control the rate of turn and the boat does capsize again, at least you're right there next to the board clinging on to it. If you've been really smart you might have rotated yourself up onto the new topside of the board, already applying your weight to it and ready to pull the boat up before the mast tip dips in the water again.

If this second capsize does occur, you should be able to recover from it because the mast won't have had time to fill up with water and the sails won't have had time to get waterlogged, So, if you're quick, you can still pull the boat upright from this second capsize quite quickly and effectively. Now with the wind on your back as you're standing on the board, it may help to release the vang and take some of the tension out of the mainsail leech.

Another tip: if you're lacking righting moment and you're standing on the board trying to get the mast out of the water, use the control line tails or spinnaker sheets to step towards the end of the board. Remember also that this extra leverage also puts additional strain on the board, so be careful if you're racing with a lightly-built foil. A broken board will make it much harder to get the boat upright, let alone what it will be like to sail with.

The other thing to remember when you're

bringing your boat upright, is to try to keep your trapeze hook away from the hull and away from the board, because it's easy to put dents in the hull and even easier to take chunks out of the fine trailing edge of the board. For this reason, it's wise to pull yourself up over the front edge of the board, so that if your hook does come into contact with the leading edge, it's unlikely to do as much damage on that side of the board.

RIGHTING FROM INVERSION

If the boat does invert, then there's a further stage that you need to get to before you go through all the steps described in the previous section.

When the boat is upside down, the hull is going to come up most easily onto its side by standing on the downwind gunwale or rack. Grasp the top of the daggerboard / centreboard and try leaning back away from the board to leeward. As the boat starts coming upright the wind should catch the underside of the hull and, if you've got solid or netted wings like a 49er or B14, the wind will catch the underside of the wings which act as a sail to start helping the boat come upright.

If the boat turns turtle, then the workload increases

WHAT IF THE MAST IS TOUCHING THE BOTTOM?

If, however, you've capsized in shallow water and you can feel or hear the mast grating on the ground, don't get on the boat, because that would just put more load on the mast. At this point the mast is very fragile and any further pressure on the mast could result in it breaking. The best thing that you can do at this stage is to help speed up the rotation of the hull around the mast until the hull is downwind and, if there's current, down tide of current. This will mean that any current and / or wind is helping push the boat downwind and helping lift the mast away from the seabed. As soon as the boat has rotated to leeward of the mast, gently put some weight on the daggerboard / centreboard and see if the boat wants to come upright.

If you can sense that it's still not wanting to come upright, then wait a little bit longer and if you think it's not going to come upright, you might want to wait for help from a rescue boat to help tow the mast tip out of the mud, or whatever it is that the mast is stuck in.

Once the mast has come clear of the mud, then you can proceed to righting the boat in the usual way.

DON'T FALL INTO THE MAINSAIL!

The first time I capsized a 49er, I jumped into the mainsail, and a split second later, I'd jumped through it! Very embarrassing, and rather expensive. If you've reached the point of no return, accept the fact and plan your exit and jump – not into the mast, not into the mainsail, but straight into the water!

RIGHT THE BOAT WITH THE KITE UP?

If you capsize in light-to-medium airs, you might be able to get the boat upright with the gennaker still hoisted. If you can get away with it, you'll be up and running much quicker than if you spend time with the boat on its side while you get the kite back into the chute. In stronger winds there are no short cuts, but it's worth experimenting with what you can get away with in light winds.

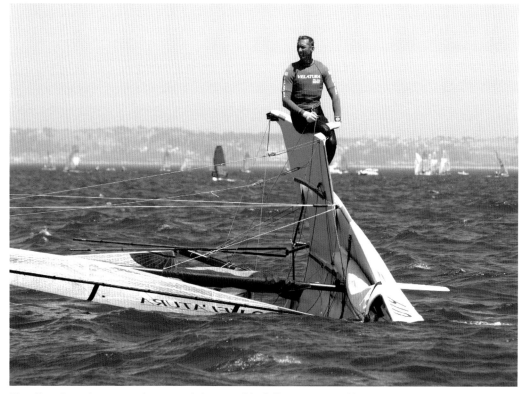

Hey, if you're going to capsize, you might as well look like you meant it!

PART 3
MASTERCLASSES

Because asymmetric boats are so dynamic and responsive, they are quite good at telling you when they feel right.

USE THE FORCE (IN THE RUDDER)

One of the best indicators in any boat is what you feel through the rudder. It should feel balanced. When the kite is oversheeted, you can feel the lee helm in the rudder. Ease the sheet to the point of the gennaker luff curling, and you'll feel the rudder becoming more balanced.

Experiment with different mainsail trim and see what effect it has on the rudder. Ease the main and you should feel the lee helm increase. Tighten the main and you'll feel the lee helm disappear again. This is why you see asymmetrics sailing around with the mainsail on or near the centreline downwind, because it's helping bring the rudder into balance.

The rudder is your best feedback tool on the boat.

The helmsman can feel how the boat is going through the feedback from the tiller

WHICH MODE SHOULD I BE IN?

There is a big difference between 'soaking' and 'planing'. It's hard to set some general rules for every kind of asymmetric boat, but let's look again at the basic principles.

In something like an RS400 you are being blown along by the breeze up to about 10 or 12 knots of true wind. This means that if you are on a run, you want to aim deep downwind with the bowsprit pulled well back (the RS400 has a swinging bowsprit), as heading up will not give you enough extra speed to justify the extra distance you will sail.

This situation changes dramatically at 10 or 12 knots however, in so-called marginal planing conditions. At this point, it can pay to luff up 10 or 20 degrees towards the wind to promote planing.

Look around you in a race in marginal planing conditions, and you will see that there are many different angles and techniques for getting downwind at almost exactly the same speed. Some techniques are more appropriate than others at different points in a race, depending on the tactical situation you are in.

In light airs, when planing is off the agenda, in some asymmetrics it can pay to ease the tack line a few inches, heel the boat over to windward and swing the gennaker to windward and away from behind the other sails. Now you are turning the gennaker into more of a conventional spinnaker. I can't tell you it will work in all boats, but it certainly works in some, for example the RS Feva.

It pays to experiment and try lots of different ways of sailing downwind, because there is often no single right answer. Get comfortable with sailing high and fast, and low and slow because they are both important skills to have in your armoury.

For the rest of this chapter, we hand over to our experts who provide their own class-specific input as to what makes their kind of asymmetric boat go fast. Some of it you may find contradictory. Not all experts agree, for example, on whether or not to raise the daggerboard / centreboard downwind. So don't take their word as gospel. Use their tips as inspiration to do your own experimenting and find out what works for you and your type of boat.

Determine your mode by whether you are being driven mainly by true wind or apparent wind

PART 3

Paul Brotherton: Determining your mode

Top 49er sailor and Olympic coach, Paul Brotherton, has an interesting way of determining which mode you should be in.

> *The important thing to understand with asymmetric rigs is when you are being blown along by the wind and when you are sailing under apparent wind. The crossover is quite stark and calls for different techniques. One of the best ways to tell whether you are apparent wind sailing or being blown by the real wind is to pull the mainsail in. If there is an immediate and large effect, then you are apparent wind sailing. If not, then you are being blown by the breeze.*

EXPERT ADVICE

Dave Hivey: Boatspeed in medium-performance hiking dinghies

Dave answers my questions.

Q **In the RS200 and RS400 fleets you're doing windward / leeward courses most of the time. So how do you achieve the best VMG?**

ANSWER: "First you've got to hot it up to get the speed in the first place. But once you go high, a lot of people then stay high. What you've got to do is, once your apparent wind starts to shift forwards, then bring it down, trim your sails accordingly with that. This means your sails are actually overtrimmed to what they should be.

I tend to get a really uneasy feeling around my stomach and the boat starts to feel a bit light when it starts to drop off the plane. And the easy thing to do then is just to shove the rudder, or to do nothing about it, and the boat drops right off the plane. You have to come all the way back up again and just try to get it planing again.

What you really should do in that situation, when you're sat down, is the crew and the helm move together if possible. But certainly for me, being the bigger bloke on most of the boats that I sail, is to drop the weight onto my toes, ease the mainsail a little bit, because my apparent wind has shifted. Then use the leeward heel of the boat to bring it up to the wind ever so slightly to hold the boat planing – and then you can steer it back down again. If you do nothing initially, you've got to stop and start all over again. If you do that continually down the run, that will cost you a hundred metres by the bottom."

Q **You said something that's probably counter-intuitive there to most people – easing the main, when you might be thinking you actually need to sheet the mainsail in to keep the power on. Does it feel like the right thing to do?**

ANSWER: *"No, not at all. It's a very, very strange thing to do and I don't think there are very many people that do it really. I only really got the hang of it fairly late in the RS200. That thing when the apparent wind starts to shift back again to ease the main and then to come back up again is, well, it's quite a weird thing to do really."*

Large mainsail, small kite means more emphasis on correct mainsail trim in the RS200

Q **And that's the main reason for having those telltales stuck on the mainsail, is it?**

ANSWER: "Yes. My problem was I was always quite slow downwind. I was always very, very quick upwind and very slow downwind. So my nickname in the fleet was 'road blocker', I was that slow downwind. But I needed to spend a lot more time working on my downwind boatspeed. And, in an asymmetric boat, it gets really difficult just to know where to set the mainsail. You can pull it in two or three feet sometimes and it doesn't seem to have any noticeable effect, although it does actually make a difference. And by having those telltales up and setting the low ones for your mainsheet and the upper ones for your kicker [vang] makes a big difference. On the RS200 the kite isn't that big. It's not a masthead sail. So there's still quite a lot of drive being taken from the main and certainly a lot of drag being taken from the main if it's not in the right position."

One of the other differences between a RS200 or 400 and most other asymmetrics is that they have pivoting centreboards rather than straight up-and-down daggerboards. So what do you do with the centreboard downwind?

ANSWER: "I leave it all the way down unless it's very, very light. So if we're on real, real soaking mode and only in flat water. The challenge with the 200 is that they're very twitchy, quite difficult to sail in soaking conditions to keep the boat dead, dead flat, or even slightly heeled to windward to float the kite round. But if you can do that and lift the centreboard up halfway as well, you can gain some serious depth downwind. Robbie Burns is exceptionally good at doing that. I don't know how he keeps his boat that well balanced downwind. It's ridiculous with the centreboard almost all the way up but he gains so much depth downwind."

So why doesn't everyone do it?

ANSWER: "It's very tricky. You need to use very, very subtle body movements over every single wave and every single gust and if you don't do it well, it's worse than not doing it the first place. For the helm, unless you're very competent in moving your shoulders at exactly the right time, it's counter-productive, because the kite will collapse almost continuously. As soon as you start to get any chop or waves then it becomes very difficult to pull it off. Actually, the safest thing to do most of the time so you don't end up collapsing your kite, is to just leave the centreboard down."

How low can you go when soaking in displacement mode, what's the limiting factor there?

"In my opinion, the limiting factor is when the jib starts to drop back across – that's your limit. So, if you can take the boat as low as you can, have a slight bit of windward heel to float the kite around windward. The lowest point you can go is when the jib starts to drop back across to windward. In these conditions I like my crew to play the kite with one hand to hold the jibsheet in the other. If the jib starts to back, they give it a little flick back again straight away. As soon as the jib pops across, it kills the flow in the kite. So that's your limit, you're always fighting on that line really, but it's worth doing. You have to sail it that low, otherwise you sacrifice so much depth."

Use the jib as your 'burgee' to indicate how low you can sail in soaking mode

EXPERT ADVICE

Rick Perkins: Boatspeed in high-performance skiffs

Now Rick answers my questions.

Q **Going in a straight line, just going flat out fast in a Musto Skiff. How do you do it?**

ANSWER: *"Well let's assume we're in a trapezing breeze, it's very much about feel and trim. Get yourself out on the trapeze, get your foot in the strap so you feel nice and stable and comfortable on the wire. Get your shoulders back into the harness. Make sure you're getting maximum leverage and then trim your mainsail in fairly close to the centreline of the boat so you're opening up the slot between the spinnaker and the mainsail and then just trimming the kite to find the sweet spot.*

That sweet spot will vary depending on different classes, but I find that I'm constantly easing to get the front of the asymmetric kite just lifting and then trimming back on. Ease the trim back on and just feel for when things are right. Keeping your body tilted back and just steering gently, keeping a nice neutral helm.

When it gets a bit lighter and you're not trapezing, then you've got the challenge of trying to decide which mode is going to be the quickest in terms of VMG. It can be very tempting to sail a bit higher and see if you can get yourself out on the wire, but then you're going to be sailing a greater distance. So learn by looking at the other boats around you and experimenting perhaps outside of racing to try to find what the best modes in different wind speeds are for your particular class. It always surprises me how going fast tends to yield the best VMG. So if you're in a sort of transitional phase where you're not sure whether to get on a wire and sail a bit further, I generally find that higher and faster is the best option. If you've got a choice where you could sit on the side of the boat and soak low or you could head up a bit and sail a further distance out on the trapeze. Typically, I find that in the Musto

Skiff, *it's preferable to take the longer distance at the higher speed. But that's not going to be the case for every class.*

In a Musto Skiff the difference between when it's in displacement mode and when it's planing in terms of boatspeed is enormous. You could perhaps go from like 6 knots to 12 knots or even more. So that's a huge difference in boatspeed whereas perhaps with another boat the difference between going high and fast and low and slow in terms of absolute boatspeed through the water is probably not so great. In the lighter boats I think the tendency would always be to try to search for the high-speed option."

Full pace in a Musto Skiff

Q **In terms of trimming the kite, is it always just have it on the curl?**

ANSWER: *"Yes, the only time that I would deviate from that is if I'm wanting to slow the boat down because of a wave set or fear of crashing. So, typically, I'm trying to keep the kite on the curl, just like I would with a conventional spinnaker."*

Q And then from what you've just said, occasionally you'll overtrim the kite and use it as a brake. You'll slow yourself down intentionally?

ANSWER: *"Yes, if you're wanting to moderate speed because of a wave set or because you've got a port-starboard situation, oversheeting the kite is just like taking your foot off the gas."*

Q And then mainsail trim, how do you know when it's trimmed right?

ANSWER: *"If you've got the mainsail out too far, the mainsail will effectively choke the slot between the two sails. A common mistake that new people in the Musto Skiff make is, they do their hoist and they get out on the wire, but they've forgot to trim the main on. So the boat is kind of less balanced because the main is out, it's slower because it's choking the slot. It's also because the head of the mainsail is a long way out, and so is pushing the bow down as well. It's much better for your straight-line speed to pull the mainsail in. In terms of a reference, if the end of the boom is over the rear quarter of the hull, that's roughly where you need to be and you can trim the mainsail depending on how you're doing in terms of height.*

So for instance, if you're wanting to, if you've understood the layline and you want to sail up a bit higher, you can ease a bit of mainsheet which will enable you to sail the boat higher to the wind with the mainsail eased. And, in extreme cases, if you're really wanting to try to make the mark, you can ease the main further. You have to beware that you can get your boat set up into quite an unstable state at that point – in that you can get yourself into almost an involuntary gybe. All of the power is in the spinnaker ahead of the mast and the mainsail's not really doing anything, so if you let the kite flog there's a danger of losing all the power in the rig and capsizing to windward."

Q So there's something a little bit counter-intuitive there for some people, when you talk about wanting to point up higher. If you want to make a gybe mark or something, you're actually easing the main whereas most of the time when you think about trying to get up higher you're thinking about pulling the mainsail in. But actually, downwind with an asymmetric it's the opposite with the mainsail, is that right? If you want to go low, you pull the mainsail in further?

ANSWER: *"Yes, as you sail higher the boat will power up. If you were sitting on the side you sail a bit higher so you can get on the wire, and if you sail higher the boat powers up even more. If you're desperately trying to make a buoy or a layline you can lose some of that power by dropping the mainsail off, but it does make the boat pretty unbalanced. One of the ways you can counteract that is to sail the boat heeled. Also, because you're going a little bit slower, the apparent wind comes further back. It's always important to have the mainsheet accessible when you're going in a straight line so you can trim it, especially for the lighter sailors. I suspect I trim my mainsail a little bit more than some of the heavier guys."*

Use the mainsheet as your height / depth control: pull it in to sail deeper, ease to sail higher

EXPERT ADVICE *continued*

Rick Perkins: Boatspeed in high-performance skiffs
Now Rick answers my questions.

Q **What do you do with the daggerboard downwind?**

ANSWER: *"I never touch it. It goes in when we launch and it comes out when I come back. The only time I ever touch the daggerboard is when it's really, really windy. I might raise it a few inches prior to the start and that's really to improve what's going on upwind. It takes the power out of the foils. I have seen people in very light winds trying to lift the centreboard or daggerboard to try to help them to soak even further downwind, but my experience is that it doesn't really make much difference. You tend to get all sorts of bits of string tangled around it, plus also because the boom is low you've got to fiddle around with it when you're gybing. So, on balance, I think it's a question of leave it down and forget about it."*

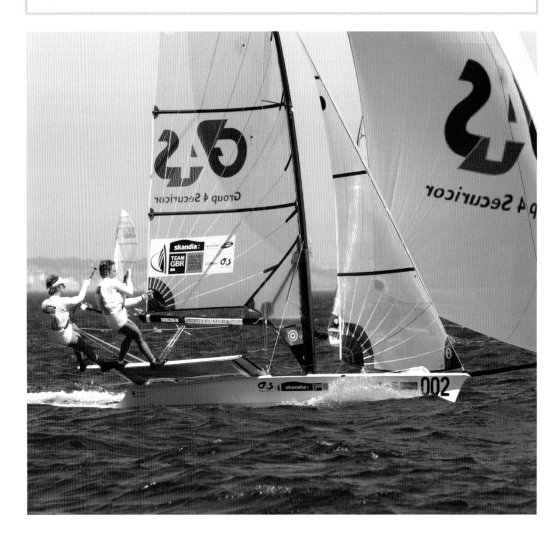

In high-performance boats that are difficult to sail well, it's vital to have good boat handling. Until you have reached a reasonable level of control over your boat, it's hard to apply tactics and strategy to your game plan on the race course. If you're still struggling to stay upright on basic manoeuvres such as tacking and gybing – and, believe me, I've been there with the 49er and Musto Skiff – then your game plan is to execute as few manoeuvres as possible. Maybe even start on port tack behind the fleet so that you can one-tack the first beat, go for a straight hoist (no gybe-set yet), slightly overstand the layline for the leeward gate so you know you can make it in one gybe. Then one-tack the next beat, and so on.

Even some of the best sailors pursue this strategy

Good tactics help you execute your race strategy

of simplicity. As they say: 'Keep It Simple Stupid!' And the KISS approach can work very well in fast asymmetrics where mistakes are so easy to make. The heavy-air finesse can come later.

STRATEGY & TACTICS

It can be easy to confuse tactics with strategy, so for the sake of clarity here are some definitions. At least, they're my definitions!

Strategy is the big picture, your pre-start plan. It's what you would do if there were no other boats on the race course. Good strategic planning involves looking at the effects on the race course such as any current, land effects, the prevailing wind, the weather forecast for the period of the race and so on. Before the start you should have a sense of what your strategy will be for sailing around the race track as fast as possible.

Tactics is how you interact with the other boats on the race course. You want to be able to execute your strategy as closely as possible to your original

plan, but other boats get in the way of that plan, especially if their strategy is similar to yours (which it often is!). So tactics are the short-term decisions that you make in order to negotiate your way as smoothly as possible around your rivals on the race course.

Getting the balance right between strategy and tactics is one of the great skills of competitive sailing. Let's say you're heading into the final race of a championship and it's down to you and another boat *Rival*. All you need to do is finish within five places of *Rival*. If there is stronger current heading upwind on the left-hand side of the course, but *Rival* tacks off to the right, which way do you go? Broadly speaking, strategy says go left for the favourable current, tactics says go right to cover *Rival*. Which is the right answer? Well, we probably don't have enough information to make that decision, but the important thing is to understand the difference between the demands of strategy and tactics.

STRATEGY & TACTICS FOR ASYMMETRICS

The faster a boat travels through the water, the more expensive each manoeuvre becomes. A fast skiff like a 49er slows to a fraction of its speed through a tack. A slow boat like a Laser / ILCA dinghy, on the other hand, loses barely any speed through a tack (at least not the way the Olympic sailors tack a Laser), so the price of each manoeuvre is much less expensive.

Boats lose less speed gybing, although in steady breezes you still want to keep your gybes to a minimum.

So can you start to see the importance of what we said earlier about having good boat-handling skills? The better and faster you can execute your basic manoeuvres, the more you can afford to make, and the more strategic and tactical decisions become available to you.

Let's start looking at some of the factors that feed into your strategic and tactical game plan, and how they will affect your decision making.

The better your boat handling, the wider your tactical options

GUSTS ARE KING

As mentioned earlier, the way that an asymmetric gennaker works is by harnessing the power of apparent wind. We have also learnt how important it is to find the strongest wind to create the most efficient airflow across your gennaker. With that in mind, you must remember that, above all else, gusts are king. Looking for dark water when you're sailing downwind is vital in any form of sailboat racing, but in high-performance asymmetric boats, it is almost without exception the most important thing that you can do.

The difference between finding that extra gust of 2 or 3 knots of breeze on one side of the course compared with your competitors in slightly less breeze, can result in hundreds of metres gain in a very short time. So, one of the key things is to look over your shoulder, but not as far behind you as you would on most conventional boats. Growing up in slow boats, most of us have learnt to look over our rear shoulder, past the transom to see where the next puffs of wind are going to reach the boat. But if your boatspeed is close to true wind speed, then you need to change your perspective.

In fast asymmetrics, now that we're sailing across the wind and we're also sailing much faster in relation to the wind speed, we need to be looking over our forward shoulder and seeing where the wind is going to reach us from abeam of the boat, rather than behind us.

In extreme cases, where you're sailing very high-performance asymmetrics and you're even exceeding true wind speed, then you actually need to be looking forward of the beam, maybe 45 degrees to windward of the bow, much as you might do when you're looking for gusts upwind. It's quite possible that the gust you encounter at the top of the windward leg, you could then meet a second time on the way downwind as you overtake the same gust!

When you're moving into asymmetrics from slower boats, it can take a lot of experience to get a sense of when the gust is going to hit, but certainly, the most important thing is to understand that the wind is going to reach you from a lot further forwards than you're used to. It might also mean that you find the wind or the gusts take a lot longer to reach you than you expect, because you're sailing away from the gusts coming up behind you.

When boatspeed exceeds wind speed, you need to be looking forward of the beam for the next gust

STAYING IN THE GUST

If the wind is gusting in streaks, rather than uniformly across the course, it pays to get into the stronger streak and stay in it as long as possible. If you can see a gust out to one side of you, arc the boat up and sail faster towards it. Once you are in the gust, bear away and soak a little more so that you stay in the gust as long as possible. And even gybe if you think that will keep you sailing in the gust for longer.

EXPERT ADVICE

Ben Saxton: Looking for the best wind

Make sure you're looking in the right direction for the breeze, which depends on wind strength but also the type of boat you're sailing. In a slower asymmetric you're looking diagonally backwards and upwind, basically off the back corner of the boat, whereas in a fast skiff you're looking over your front shoulder to look for the gybe that you're on, and looking backwards and square for the breeze that you'd get if you went on to the other gybe.

Pressure is the most important factor in fast boats because when you get the gust you go a lot lower and it's very hard to tell whether you're in better pressure or a better shift; you can see pressure on the water and it's harder to see shift. Seeing windshifts gets easier in bigger fleets because you can compare your heading to the bulk of the boats across the race course. And it's also useful to look at the headings of any boats going upwind as an indicator of what the shift might be doing downwind.

EXPERT ADVICE

Chris Nicholson: Looking for the wind

My general impression is that a lot of skiff sailors look too far behind them. In a 49er or an 18-foot Skiff, my angle of focus would be about 45 degrees to windward of the bow. Look much further behind you than that, and the breeze you're looking at may never reach you. Basically, the faster your boat, the further forward you need to be looking to see the breeze that will affect you.

I also look to leeward in a fairly wide arc to see what breeze I can expect to pick up when I gybe. I don't find it too easy to work out the breeze I'm going to be in when I've gybed, so this is why my point of focus is wider. But I think in a 49er you should be looking out beyond the aft quarter for an idea of what to expect after the gybe.

You want to look for the darkest water and aim to pick that breeze up. If you can see lighter water ahead and to windward, then you need to be looking over your shoulder to see if you'll be getting more wind if you gybe. In bright sunlight, when the sun can make it quite hard to pick out the strength and direction of the breeze, I use polarised sunglasses as these really help bring out the contrast in dark and light on the water.

It can pay to swing a little higher on the trapeze to help you look around more easily at what's going on. I'd guess I spend around 30 to 40 percent of my time looking around. 49ers are difficult to make sure they're going at 100 percent pace all the time, but it's worth sacrificing a bit of all-out speed to keep an eye on the bigger picture.

Finding the strongest breeze remains the priority until the boat is going really fast in strong wind. Then, angle of breeze gets more important. Knowing how to weigh up the relative merits of gusts and shifts is really down to experience.

Look over your front shoulder for the next breeze

Rick Perkins: Sailing in clear air is fast

> Sailing in clear air is fast. It's an obvious statement, but it's crucial to bear it in mind when sailing asymmetrics downwind.

Because wind pressure makes such a difference to boatspeed, and because you have such a narrow angle for achieving optimum speed, it's worth carving yourself a lane where you can sail the boat how you want to sail it. Sailing in a big fleet, sailing in the pack is pretty slow compared to just having a bit of free space and doing your own thing. That's why the gybe-set often works out well for people, because they have the space to do their own thing over on the left-hand side whereas the bulk of the fleet tends to go to the right. People can often make up good ground, not because it was the correct side of the run to go, but because they've just been sailing the natural fast angles, whereas everyone else has been sailing non-optimum angles defending their lane: those sailing in clear air are getting top speed out of their boats.

Ben Saxton: Create space around you

> *Space, for me, is a golden rule downwind. Generally, I do whatever it takes to build space around me, to get clear air. If the fleet's generally going high, going low often isn't a good move because you're likely to be in dirty wind for a long time. So generally I'd go high, make the VMG gains and then a minute or two before you want to gybe, you start soaking down to other people's lines with the speed that you've gained. So then you're free for the gybe. Because normally once you've made the gain forward, you can translate that into 'down', if you want to.*
>
> *It's worth pushing a mode if it's going to gain you space. For example, if you've just gybed and someone else has gybed on you, it might be worth pushing forward to get clear ahead of them. Or you want to really soak down while the boat above you might end up fighting with the boat above it that has gybed on them. So you soak for a bit, then 20 seconds later, once you've created the gap, you go into high mode with loads of space again, and you accelerate into clear air, never to be seen again!*

THE WINDWARD MARK

START LOOKING FOR THE GUST EARLY

So, if we're going to find the darkest water to get the strongest gust, then we need to start planning how we're going to catch that first gust from well before we reach the windward mark. Start looking upwind and look at the water to windward of the windward mark. Make a decision where you think the strongest wind is going to be and what manoeuvre is going to take you most quickly to that dark line of breeze.

As you look upwind, if it's to the left of the windward mark, then a straight set should do it nicely; just bear away, hoist, and sail into that gust. But if, as you look upwind, the best darkest breeze looks like it's on the right, then not only might you experience a little bit of that gust as you approach the windward mark, but the quickest way to harness that gust once you've hoisted the gennaker is by executing a gybe-set manoeuvre.

LIFT OR HEADER?

One of the other tell-tale signs to look out for as you're approaching the windward mark is whether you're on a header or a lift as you approach the mark. If you're on your final starboard approach to the mark and you find yourself being lifted above the layline, then a lift on starboard would mean that you would want to gybe set so that you get that same change in wind direction, creating a header on port gybe.

Remember that, just as you want to make the most of the lifts on the windward leg, you want to make the most of the headers on the downwind leg, because it's the headers that take you closer to the leeward mark.

If, on the other hand, you find yourself being headed as you approach the windward mark and you're struggling to even get around the windward mark, then this is a tell-tale sign that opting for a straight hoist and remaining on starboard gybe would be a good thing.

GETTING INTO POSITION AT THE WINDWARD MARK

Another factor to consider in your tactics is your positioning relative to the rest of the fleet. Remember that your primary goal is to get into the strongest wind. So for example, if you encounter good strong wind up the right-hand side of the course as you approach the windward mark, then you know that you want to be gybe setting to be able to capture that new wind really early on the downwind leg. This means you want to be in position to complete the gybe-set without fouling other boats. So plan ahead and start booking your space for an inside rounding at the windward mark.

If you've been approaching the layline from quite high and other boats are running into you on their approach to the layline, then you have some work to do here. Rather than racing to try to get over the top of the boats just to leeward of you, it might pay to slow down, let them go and create a space in the line around the windward mark. This will mean that you are clear to gybe immediately as you pass the windward mark and get into that strong tactical gybe-set position.

On the other hand, if the best breeze is to be found by doing a straightforward bear-away then

Plan your downwind leg well before you get to the windward mark

Where you tack on the layline will determine where you can sail down the run

you will need to negotiate the majority of the fleet also setting their gennakers on starboard.

Now there are other considerations. Largely what you do next is determined by how long you have until you need to gybe. If you are on a short course and you are expecting to gybe in the next two or three minutes then you want to make sure that you are in a position to be able to do that gybe when you choose to. It may not pay you to pull off a fast efficient hoist and get up on the windward hip of another boat unless you can get up and around the front of him in time for your gybe.

Instead, it may be better to hold fire on your fastest hoist and aim to dive down low to match the line of that boat in front. Even better if you can dive lower to leeward of his line – because this puts you in the controlling position to be able to gybe when you want.

WHEN SHOULD I GYBE SET?

Most of the time, the straight set is the safest tactical call, particularly at the first windward mark when there's a lot of traffic. Also, from a boat-handling perspective, gybe setting is a tricky manoeuvre to get right. But there can be great tactical reasons for giving it a go. Here are five factors that might tempt you to make that early gybe.

1. More Wind

By now you should already appreciate the importance of stronger wind when you're sailing dynamic and responsive asymmetric boats. Of course, if the wind is blowing really hard, then staying upright is the priority and pulling off a gybe-set can be a tricky manoeuvre. So you have to balance your tactical considerations against your boat-handling ability. Better to hoist, set, then gybe when you're up to full pace if you're worried about falling in.

More wind is the best reason to gybe early

2. Windshifts

Hooking into an extra 3 or 5 knots of breeze is by far the most important consideration in an asymmetric boat, but if the wind strength is even across the course, think next about windshifts. If you are approaching the windward mark on a nice starboard lift, you will want to gybe to take advantage of the same shift which, once you're going downwind, will be a port header. If a header up the end of the beat made it hard to make the windward mark on starboard tack, that is your cue to go for a straight set and hoist the gennaker on starboard.

If you pick up a starboard lift which is also gusting, then you will most likely want to gybe straightaway. Your angles can change massively in this scenario, and you may find that you are almost pointing at the leeward mark once you have gybed. If you carry on and hoist onto starboard in this lifting gust situation, you are in danger of overstanding the layline and losing ground to those who gybe set behind you.

3. Tidal Considerations

If there is current or tide on the course, then remember that what helps you upwind hinders you downwind, and vice versa. So be aware of the state of the tide around each mark and consider your tactics accordingly.

4. Where Is The Fleet?

We've thought about some strategic factors, now let's think about some tactical, boat-to-boat considerations. If you're rounding the windward mark for the first time, in the front half of the fleet, chances are there'll be a line of boats behind you on the starboard layline. This creates a big wind shadow in the area just to leeward, so you have to have a really good case for gybe setting in this situation.

If you've just been enjoying that big starboard-lifting gust we talked about earlier, then go for that gybe-set, and you'll soon be out of that nasty wind hole. Short-term pain for long-term gain. Otherwise, hoist on starboard and sail for at least 100 metres before making your first gybe. That way, you'll avoid the worst of the disturbed air. But if you're in the back half of the fleet, the wind hole won't be so great, so you can revert to your strategic priorities.

5. Nothing To Lose

If you're right at the back and running out of time to make up places in the race, then your best bet is often to do the opposite to what most of the fleet is doing. As at least three-quarters of the fleet usually does a straight hoist on starboard, you have nothing to lose in gybe setting and seeing if you pick up a 'gust from heaven' on the left-hand side of the course.

You've really got nothing to lose in this situation, because unless a load of boats capsize, you're unlikely to overtake them going the same way. Might as well gybe and roll the dice for a bit of luck!

Nothing to lose – do something different

Steve Irish: Get on to the 'long gybe'

Most of the time you will find the majority of the fleet will do a straight set on starboard, because the gybe-set's quite a risky manoeuvre. So then your consideration is: which is your 'long gybe'? In other words, which gybe you will be on for longer? If the long gybe is starboard then you might go for the roll or stay higher or just hold your lane. You need to maintain clear air as long as possible. If it's actually the long gybe on port then you're going to be looking for a soak, so the set needs to be low. This will give you control over your point of gybe, to set you up for clear air on the long gybe.

JUDGING LAYLINES

Judging laylines in an asymmetric boat can be very tricky, especially if the wind is unstable, because you would have already discovered just how much variations in wind strength and wind direction can affect the direction of your boat.

Laylines can move around with every gust and lull

If it is lighter winds, then it may pay to overstand the layline. This means that you keep lots of apparent wind running over the sails as you approach the leeward mark, and anybody who is coming in a little bit too high and a little bit too deep will pay a high price with vastly reduced boatspeed. Remember, gennakers are hugely efficient sails, but only when they have flow across the sail. Coming in too high in light winds will kill your boatspeed.

So make sure that you are not one of those boats trying to run too deep with a limp gennaker. Make sure that you are one of the ones coming in hotted up and with lots of speed into that leeward mark, because your apparent wind will carry you through the dirty air of the slow boats to windward.

If you do find that you are coming into a leeward mark a little too high and you are starting to run deep, look around you, and make a decision about whether you should cut your losses early and put in two more gybes to get down to the mark. In light winds, the loss of distance from two gybes is minimal, and the boat handling is relatively straightforward. More often than not it's better to go for the double gybe than blob along with a floppy gennaker.

In stronger winds, this is a bigger decision

because you lose more distance through a gybe compared with your straight-line speed. Not only that, there's also the risk of capsizing. So you really have to make this decision based on your confidence and your ability to gybe effectively.

With that in mind, we've already said that generally in light winds it pays to overstand the gybe mark in light airs. The same is often true in strong airs because, rather than facing the two extra gybes and the risk of broaching or capsizing, it can be better to overstand the layline. It might mean that you have to drop the gennaker earlier and do some two-sail reaching to get back up to the leeward mark. But that may be a price worth paying compared with the risk of those two extra gybes and a resulting possible capsize.

Are you starting to see how the quality of your boat handling affects the quality of your tactical decisions?

EXPERT ADVICE

Chris Nicholson: When to gybe for the layline

" *Obviously, as you approach the layline, your time for gybing is running out. In most conditions I like to try to gybe a little bit early of the layline so that I can still get back to the centre of the course. In light winds you can sometimes get away with overstanding a little bit, as other boats above you try to soak too low to get to the mark. But be careful. Take a careful check of the pressure across the course before making this crucial gybe.*

In strong winds, bear in mind it could take some time to get the gybe in safely, especially if there's a big seaway, so aim to get your gybe in earlier than you might think. When it's windy, don't be too sad if one or two boats roll you, just so long as you keep on moving – and stay upright!" "

TIDAL CONSIDERATIONS

These differ very little from those in other conventional spinnaker boats, except that the potential for gain or loss in, say, a strong tidal situation is much greater. This is because your separation across the course from one side to the other is much larger than on boats with spinnaker poles that tend to stick closer to the rhumb line. If you are going down the run with the tide running with you, you can afford to gybe early even if you find yourself soaking to the mark, as the tide will carry you there. Far better to do that than gybe late

and find you're having to tight-reach back to the mark as the tide tries to sweep you off downwind.

On the other hand, with the tide running against you down the run, you are safer to overstand on your final gybe, and come in towards the leeward mark with pace and control. There's nothing worse than running deeper and deeper towards the leeward mark against an adverse tide. The more you bear away the less efficient the gennaker becomes, and you often see people wrapping themselves around the leeward mark as a result. And that can ruin your day.

LEEWARD TURN

LEEWARD MARK

With a leeward mark, on a normal port-rounding course, all other things being equal, aim to approach it on starboard gybe. This gives you rights on other boats on pretty much every count. Outside of the three boat-lengths' circle, and you hold precedence on the basic port-starboard rule, and inside the three boat lengths you have room on boats outside of you.

LEEWARD GATE

With a leeward gate, things are a bit more complicated. The leeward rounding in short-course asymmetric racing is one of the most crucial parts of the race. If you're in the front pack, you need to think ahead and defend your position around the mark. If you're behind, this is your main opportunity in the race to attack and get back into the leading pack.

Keeping moving is the key to escaping the leeward gate

EXPERT ADVICE

Chris Draper: The leeward gate

I spoke to Chris Draper, Olympic medallist and double World Champion in the 49er, about his approach to this crucial phase of the race. He's talking about a leeward gate, although many of the same principles apply with a single leeward mark.

Keep on moving – *The overriding factor with the leeward rounding is to get in and out of that area as fast as possible because it's such a stopping point. It's the only time in the race where boats really tend to slow down, so you want to minimise your 'down time'.*

I think there's a good analogy here with when you're driving on the road and you want to overtake a car on a single-lane carriageway. You want to sit a little distance back from them, so that when your overtaking opportunity arrives you can use run-up speed to get past them, and spend the minimum time on the opposite side of the road. It's similar with the leeward mark; the more speed you come in with on your approach, the better the chance you have of getting out of there quickly too.

Think ahead – *Because the leeward rounding is so important, in some cases we'll start to think about it even before we've rounded the windward mark. Normally, we'll sail past the gate at the start to check if there is any heavy bias, and we'll make a mental note about which one is favoured. Also, if we think one side of the course is favoured, we'll make a plan to round the mark that takes us out to that side.*

If we want the left-hand mark (looking downwind), we might even think about a gybe-set at the windward mark. We've got a number of processes we'll go through when making our plan. But that plan could change depending on whether we're in attacking mode (i.e. looking to gain places) or defending mode (already in a top position).

If we're defending, we'll aim to make a fast windward mark rounding and to get to the leeward gate as quickly as possible. This might sound obvious, but this gets much harder when you're attacking, when there are many more things to think about.

When you've got space around you, and the luxury of selecting either leeward mark, you want to take the one that will get you out to what you expect will be the favoured side of the next windward leg. This means looking back upwind before your drop the gennaker, to see if there are any useful puffs or shifts coming down either side of the course.

Think ahead before the decision is made for you

Traffic avoidance – *However, once you've got other boats to contend with, which more often than not you do, then your priorities can change dramatically. If you've got a lot of traffic queuing up to go around one mark, then it can pay to go around the other one even when it's further to sail there. Remember your No.1 rule of getting in and out of this area ASAP.*

If we're in attacking mode and wanting to come into the mark fast, we'll aim to come in tight

EXPERT ADVICE **Chris Draper: The leeward gate** (Continued)

on the layline with speed, and with rights at the mark, and usually aim for a gybe-drop inside the boats that are queuing up there. Remember that in an asymmetric boat, which sails wide angles downwind, you can establish rights on other boats sometimes from hundreds of metres away, because you're overlapped the whole way down.

But bear in mind that if you're aiming for a gybe-drop inside other boats, your boat handling had better be good. The better your boat handling, the more aggressively you can deal with the leeward mark situation. Good boat control gives you more tactical options.

Make sure that you plan well ahead. You can see plenty of people who only make their minds up about which leeward mark at the very last minute, but we do everything we can to avoid this. We rarely change our minds into the leeward gate; we'll discuss it a long way out and try very hard to avoid a situation where you have to make a spontaneous decision. Far better to make a solid plan than to be dictated to by other people, simply because you failed to think ahead.

Thinking ahead is the key to success, when trying to break through the log jam at the leeward gate

Going for the favoured side – *If you know that one side of the beat is favoured, and everyone else does too, then you know you've got a fight on your hands to get round the favoured leeward mark – unless, of course, you're in the lead. If we're quite forward in the fleet, and just looking to pick off the odd boat or two, we might accept going around the favoured mark and hanging on to the same line as the leaders out of the mark.*

But if we are looking to make big gains (i.e. we're further back in the fleet), then it might be worth taking the wrong leeward mark and then putting in an early tack over to the favoured side. This way, you'll have your own lane across to the favoured side. In a fast skiff like a 49er when you sail faster you go higher too, so you have the opportunity to sail past boats that are just 'chopping wood' [Draper-speak for boats that are pinching up and going slow as they see-saw through the waves].

However, if you have only got one boat in the queue ahead of you round the favoured mark, it can pay to foot out low from the leeward mark and grab some clean air ahead and to leeward. Of course, if there are other boats further ahead, then this isn't so good because you'll be gasping for air.

When you're racing to establish three boat-lengths' rights with another boat, it can pay to hang on late to the kite, just so you get around in front of your rival. The crew can finish off the kite drop once you've rounded the mark with your nose in front. But, again, get out of there as quick as you can, and leave any non-vital tidying until you're fully sorted and up to speed away from the mark.

Judging laylines – Judging laylines in asymmetric boats can be tricky, but the biggest priority here is to make sure you're approaching the leeward mark at speed. You don't want to sail slow, and we'll avoid soaking to the mark in all situations except for the very lightest of breezes, say 2-3 knots or less, because the drop in boatspeed is proportionally much less significant.

If it's windy, I'll look back up the middle of the course to see what pressure is coming when we gybe and use that to gauge my most likely layline. Once we've gybed, my crew will take a transit on the mark and tell me how we're doing on it. His feedback will dictate how I steer to the mark. If it's very windy, we'll tend not to put in a gybe-drop, because that would be a very high-risk option that we'd rather avoid.

We've talked about what you should do, but just to emphasise some critical points, here is a quick list of don'ts:

Don't

- Soak to the mark – do an extra gybe instead (or get your layline right in the first place!)
- Think too late – make an early decision
- Get stuck on the outside of a mark rounding – make sure you've got rights at the mark.

The *Racing Rules of Sailing* have been around for a long time, and have been written primarily with slower boats in mind, which tend to sail directly from A to B.

Because the new breed of high-performance boats with asymmetric gennakers travel faster and gybe through wider angles downwind, this makes it important to understand some of the implications when you bring the Racing Rules into the equation.

One of the nice aspects of fast asymmetric boats is that kinetics such as pumping, ooching and rocking tend not to have much of an effect on boatspeed. In fact it's more likely you'll disturb the air flow over the sails and slow the boat down, so the dreaded Rule 42 tends not to have much relevance.

For this section of the book I have brought in **Chris Simon**, a skilled judge and umpire with wide experience of racing at all levels of the sport, from the Volvo Ocean Race to the America's Cup to club racing.

KNOW YOUR LEFTS FROM YOUR RIGHTS

When you're looking at two gate marks, which do you call the left mark and which the right? It might sound like a stupid question, but there are two ways of looking at them and, if you're sailing on a boat with two or more people, then it's critical that everyone has the same understanding about which is left and which is right. When you're looking at a map of the course on shore in a race briefing, for example, it's fairly obvious which is left and which is right. Isn't it? Trouble is, when you're two minutes away from the leeward gate on a busy race course, when you, as the helmsman, call for a gennaker drop around the right-hand mark, exactly which one do you mean now? You might know what you mean, but does your crew?

For the purposes of our conversation with Chris Simon, Chris suggested that we call it as we see it while sailing **downwind** on the race course. So as we're sailing downwind, the mark we see on the left is the 'left' mark and the one on the right is the 'right'. Right? Good. Now we can begin.

LEEWARD GATES

EXPERT ADVICE

 The rules that govern your entry into the leeward gate zone can be very complicated, especially if the two marks are close together...

ANSWER: *"With the standard zone of three hull lengths, race management recommendation is that the separation between the marks is eight hull lengths. So the aim is to have a two boat-length*

space in the middle which is outside the zone of either mark. A problem arises if race committees lay the marks less than six lengths apart, in which case you have a sector in the middle where a boat could actually be in the zone of both marks. This can create potential rules issues, but provided the gate is set at the recommended space then, essentially, each mark can be looked at separately."

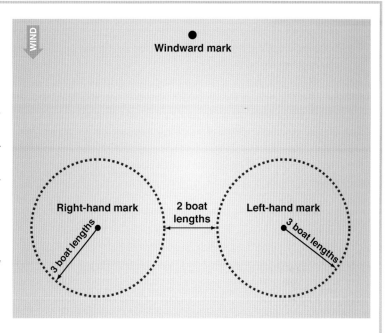

COLLISION COURSE AT LEEWARD GATE

Q OK, so let's say there are two boats on different gybes on a collision course as they're approaching the leeward gate. One boat is coming in from the right-hand side and is wanting to go round the left-hand gate, so that boat would be on port gybe; then there is another boat on starboard gybe wanting to go round the right-hand mark. Talk us through the scenario.

ANSWER: *"As they approach the gate, provided both boats are outside the zone, it is just a straight port and starboard. There is no other complication until one of them reaches the zone of a mark."*

PART 3

106

Q OK, so once the port-gybe boat enters the zone of the right-hand leeward mark, then it has rights to room at that mark. But what if for tactical reasons – say a lot of traffic and congestion at the right-hand mark – the port-gybe boat wanted to keep on heading over to the other mark on the left?

ANSWER: *"You have to make certain assumptions, and the assumption you must make is that a boat that enters the zone of a mark is treated as if it was going to round that mark. Quite frankly the other boat can't be expected to mind read. So if the boat on port comes into the zone of the right-hand mark, whether or not the starboard boat is at that time in the zone, the port-gybe boat is the inside boat and is entitled to mark-room. The fact that they're on opposite gybes doesn't matter because boats sailing downwind on opposite gybes are overlapped."*

Q So the yellow boat at the moment thinks that the blue boat is going to gybe and round inside him...

ANSWER: *"In relation to the right-hand mark, yellow is faced with an inside boat within the zone and has therefore got to give that boat mark-room. Now the port-gybe boat must give way because the normal right-of-way rule still applies, so she is a boat on port who's got to keep clear of the boat on starboard but the starboard boat has got to give mark-room to the port boat.*

Mark-room is room to sail to the mark, and I can think of one World Sailing case in particular which says 'to the mark' means that she must sail within a 'corridor' that goes from the place where she entered the zone to the position where she would begin to alter course to round the mark. Provided she is within that corridor, she is protected because Rule 43.1.b says that as long as she is taking mark-room to which she is entitled, she is exonerated for breaking another rule, in this case Rule 10, the port-starboard rule.

So the port-tack boat has got a bit of a conundrum because she actually wants to round the left-hand mark. In order to do that she has got to give way to the starboard boat, because she will not be sailing to the right-hand mark. So her exoneration from breaking the port-starboard rule would not apply if she just simply sailed straight through the zone of the right-hand mark going to the left-hand mark. The starboard boat has a clear-cut situation here, as the port boat has got to keep clear of her but she must give her mark-room. If the starboard boat sees the port-tack boat leave the corridor, in other words the port-tack boat hardens up and points at the left-hand mark, then the starboard boat is entitled to shout 'Starboard!' and to expect her to keep clear."

Q Is 'the corridor' a term that you would use in a protest scenario? Is it a recognised term?

ANSWER: *"Yes, I think it is. If you look at Case No.75 in the World Sailing Case Book, it was defined as a 'corridor'."*

WORLD SAILING CASE BOOK, CASE NO.75

Case No.75 in the World Sailing Case Book looks at a situation where two boats were sailing downwind on opposite gybes to a leeward mark. In that situation, the jury's decision says the mark-room that the port-tack boat was required to give to the starboard-tack boat was the space needed in existing conditions to sail promptly to the mark in a seamanlike way. That space was a direct corridor from the point where starboard entered the zone to a position close to and alongside the mark on the required side. So 'corridor' is a term that is actually used in that case.

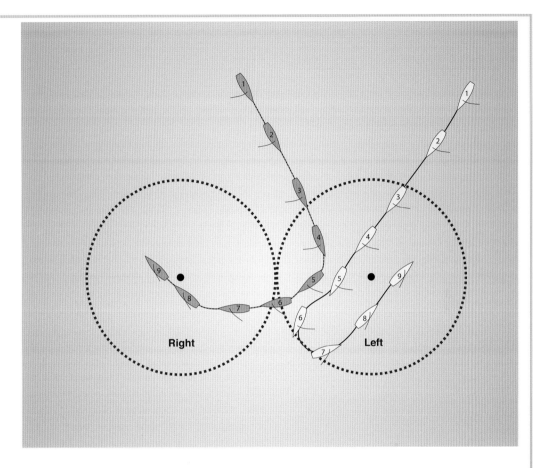

GOING AROUND THE LEFT-HAND GATE MARK

"Now, the situation if two boats are approaching the left-hand mark of a leeward gate is worth a closer look. The boat on starboard is not obliged to gybe around the mark. If she wishes, the starboard boat can cause the port boat to gybe to avoid her, and then can sail her away from that mark. The starboard boat can then gybe and round that mark if she so wishes."

 Seems a bit unfair!

ANSWER: *"Well, it certainly creates tactical opportunities! If this was a single leeward mark, then the starboard boat would be obliged to gybe in the normal way around the mark. Rule 18.4 says she shall sail no further from the mark than her proper course to gybe. But where there is a leeward gate, Rule 18.4 doesn't apply."*

 Strange that one rule should apply for a leeward mark, and another rule for a leeward gate…

ANSWER: *"A working party was tasked with coming up with a new mark rounding rule, but it was too difficult to come up with an appropriate form of words that was fair. So it's important for sailors to understand the distinction between leeward mark and leeward gate situations."*

SEAMANLIKE ROUNDING

EXPERT ADVICE

Q Some asymmetric boats are very high performance and the boat handling can be very challenging. What's the definition of 'seamanlike' when you're talking about boats that are very hard to handle such as the 49er?

ANSWER: *"Well, 'seamanlike' is not a defined term within the Racing Rules and therefore we refer to its normal English meaning. I think one could say that its normal English meaning is that the boat is handled in a competent way, and again there are one or two cases which specifically say that if the boat isn't handled in a seamanlike way then from a rules point of view, giving room or keeping clear is not extended to cater for that lack of competence. So if a boat is by definition difficult to handle, then seamanlike does assume that the people who are sailing it are doing that competently. As soon as there is an implication or an admission that it was not done competently, then I think that begins to be un-seamanlike. So you've got to look at seamanlike as being what you would expect in the upper end of the fleet – there's no concession for novices or short-handed sailors, for example."*

WINDWARD V LEEWARD BOAT

EXPERT ADVICE

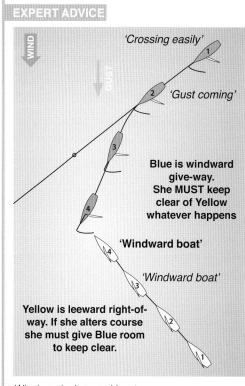

'Crossing easily'

'Gust coming'

Blue is windward give-way. She MUST keep clear of Yellow whatever happens

'Windward boat'

'Windward boat'

Yellow is leeward right-of-way. If she alters course she must give Blue room to keep clear.

WIND

GUST

Windward v leeward boats

Q So let's say we've got blue boat sailing downwind with gennaker on starboard gybe. We've got yellow boat sailing upwind on starboard tack. Now yellow boat in all situations is the right-of-way boat, but the nature of asymmetrics is that they can change course very quickly with even a slight change in wind speed. What sort of options does blue have if it suddenly gets hit by a gust and finds itself heading straight for yellow?

ANSWER: *"The only option is to keep clear, because that's what the rule demands. In this situation it's actually windward / leeward, Rule 11. Responding to a gust and keeping clear could be seen as a measure of seamanship. It is not a defence for a give-way boat to say: 'I was out of control, therefore I couldn't keep clear so I ought to be exonerated.' It's tough, simple as that. And blue in this scenario has no way out because she's on starboard, if she gybed onto port, it would give her a different angle and she'd probably get across, but it doesn't matter which way she does it – as long as she keeps clear."*

This International 14 is struggling to keep clear of the boat coming upwind

KEEPING A LOOKOUT DOWNWIND

EXPERT ADVICE

Q One of the problems is the lack of visibility with a lot of gennakers on modern-day asymmetrics, so what is the advice other than keeping a good lookout?

ANSWER: *"There have been many discussions about this, but they have all led to the same conclusion, that it is the onus of the give-way boat. In fact it is the onus on all boats, to keep a proper lookout. A boat is not excused from keeping a proper lookout because she has a sail set in a particular way which means that she doesn't have good visibility in a particular direction."*

Q What about if you're going upwind and you see a boat coming towards you? What onus is there on you, if any, to highlight to the 'blind' boat that you're there?

ANSWER: *"Well I think it raises interesting questions because Rule 14, avoiding contact, actually says a boat shall avoid contact with another boat if reasonably possible; that includes keeping a proper lookout and doing everything that's reasonable and possible to avoid contact. There is a case that looks at such a situation, where there was contact between boats just before the start.*

On each boat the bowman was involved in some sail handling and therefore neither bowman saw the other boat coming on a head-on collision course, and the boats did collide. The decision in that case was that neither boat would be exonerated because they didn't see the other boat. They were not doing everything that was reasonably possible to avoid the contact.

So going back to the situation you were talking about, I believe that a starboard-tack boat coming upwind which sees a boat coming downwind with gennaker set towards her, irrespective of whether the other boat is on port gybe or starboard gybe, the starboard close-hauled boat would be well advised to hail. If there was a collision, even though she was the right-of-way boat and even though there's nothing in the rules to say she's got to hail, it might be argued that she didn't do all that was reasonably possible to avoid the collision. So the best advice for the close-hauled boat is to hail. Better safe than sorry."

CAPSIZED BOATS

EXPERT ADVICE

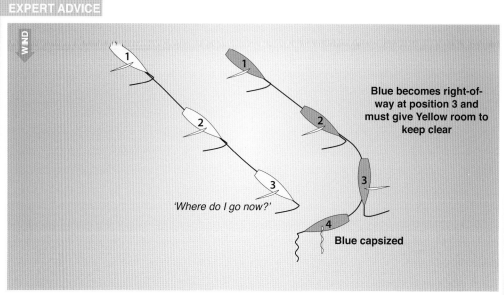

Blue becomes right-of-way at position 3 and must give Yellow room to keep clear

'Where do I go now?'

Blue capsized

Capsized boat

Q Let's say there are two boats on port, the lead boat gybed onto starboard, capsized and left the port boat nowhere to go. Who's in the right, who's in the wrong?

ANSWER: *"If we go back to basics, Rule 22 says, if possible, a boat shall avoid a boat that is capsized or has not regained control after capsizing. So in this case the boat on port, if possible, shall avoid the boat that has capsized. The fact that blue had already got onto starboard before she capsized is not actually relevant to the rules issue. So that assumes that the capsize happened when the other boat was far enough away to take avoiding action. If the capsize happens so close that it is not reasonably possible for the other boat to avoid the collision, then the upright boat will not have broken Rule 22.*

Let's look in more detail at the timing of the incident. As soon as the lead boat gybed onto starboard, in other words as soon as her boom had travelled across the centreline, she became the right-of-way boat. Can one argue that a right-of-way boat that capsizes has changed course, in other words has she broken Rule 16? In this particular case she might also have broken Rule 15 because, irrespective of the capsize, her gybe was so close that the port-tack boat couldn't take avoiding action, then she'd have broken Rule 15. This says she must initially give the newly give-way boat room to keep clear. If, on the other hand, had she not capsized, the port boat could have avoided her and was only foiled by the boat that's now on starboard capsizing, then maybe it can be argued that she's broken Rule 16.

We don't have a case, but we have a match racing call which says that a boat going ahead to going astern, or a boat that was going astern now going ahead is a change of course. So I don't think it's a very big step to go from that to saying that a boat that was sailing quickly across the bows of a give-way boat that capsizes and stops crossing the bows might also be argued to have changed course. We haven't actually got anything to rely on specifically there, but I believe that it's not an unreasonable extension of the match racing call."

GYBE-SET AT THE WINDWARD MARK

EXPERT ADVICE

Yellow's gybe, between positions 4 and 5, is part of her proper course at the mark as she is still 'overlapped' on the mark

Blue is clear astern when Yellow reaches the 3-length zone, so must give Yellow mark-room

Gybing at the windward mark

Q **When you gybe set at the windward mark on a typical port mark rounding, what rights if any do you have?**

ANSWER: *"Firstly, the hoisting and setting of the gennaker has no relevance to the rules situation. Aside from any boats coming upwind towards the windward mark, a boat's main issue is likely to be with a boat that's following close behind her. Let's say the trailing boat was clear astern when the leading boat reached the zone; therefore the trailing boat has got to give the leading boat mark-room (as she also would have to if she was overlapped outside her). There is no doubt that bearing away to a downwind course is her proper course around the mark. The question is, does gybing on to port count as part of her proper course around the mark? And I think the answer is yes, it is, provided it is done as a continuous manoeuvre. Rule 18.1 says that Rule 18 (all of it!) no longer applies when mark-room has been given. Therefore an issue arises if the leading boat – having borne away to a downwind course on starboard – delays the gybe, so that she is now clearly past the mark. If she bears away, sails in a straight line for a little bit and then bears away further and gybes, that is not covered by her mark-room rights. So during that gybe she would be going from right-of-way clear ahead to give-way port, and there it's not the action of the other boat that's caused the right-of-way to change, so she has no entitlement to room or anything else. If she is going to do that delayed gybe, she needs to keep clear throughout the manoeuvre."*

Q Let's say there's an offset mark a few boat lengths along from the windward mark – if the trailing boat has a slight overlap here, then the lead boat has no rights to gybe, right?

ANSWER: *"Again, the first question to ask is, were they overlapped at the zone of the offset mark? If they were overlapped at the zone, then the inside boat has the right to mark-room. If they were not overlapped in the zone, then the trailing boat has got to give the leading boat mark-room just as we discussed earlier."*

ANY RIGHTS WHILE GYBE SETTING?

Q In some fast boats like a 49er the best way to hoist the kite for a gybe-set is to hoist most of the kite first, and then gybe just as you've got the kite hoisted to the top of the mast. If you do this in stronger winds, you'd probably be out of the zone by the time you were gybing. So the question is, is it any defence for the lead boat to say I'm sailing my proper course because this is the way I'd gybe if I was on my own?

ANSWER: *"No, because mark-room has already been given and so no part of Rule 18 applies. So, if in this scenario, she is clearly no longer at the mark because she's now one or two boat lengths beyond it, the mark rounding rule has switched off. You're back in the land of normal right-of-way rules and, irrespective of whether or not the kite is up, her gybe will take her onto port and she will go from right-of-way starboard to give-way port. She's got no protection under Rule 15. She's got to keep clear all the time, from the moment the boom crosses the centreline."*

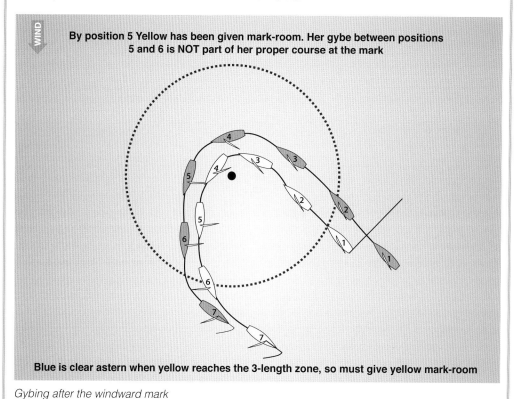

WIND

By position 5 Yellow has been given mark-room. Her gybe between positions 5 and 6 is NOT part of her proper course at the mark

Blue is clear astern when yellow reaches the 3-length zone, so must give yellow mark-room

Gybing after the windward mark

TWO SAILS AGAINST THREE SAILS ON A REACH

EXPERT ADVICE

WIND

Thereafter, Yellow may continue her luff, whether or not Blue actually took down the sail

Blue, with gennaker set, establishes an overlap to windward

At position 3, when Blue's gennaker ceases to draw, Yellow must give Blue room to drop the sail

Yellow, two-sail reaching, luffs to defend her weather

Q Some classes like the International 14 have reaches in their race courses, and there's sometimes a decision about whether or not to carry a gennaker down to the gybe mark. So let's say there's one International 14 with a gennaker up, but with a rival to leeward without gennaker, two-sail reaching to the mark. Equally well, this might happen in handicap racing against a non-asymmetric boat. Talk us through the potential issues in this scenario.

ANSWER: *"The two-sail boat is the leeward boat, the three-sail boat has established an overlap up to windward so there is no doubt the leeward boat has luffing rights, and that Rule 17 does not apply. She will be the right-of-way boat when they're overlapped: the leeward right-of-way boat altering course. So a right-of-way boat altering course has got to give room for the other boat to keep clear.*

I don't think we have got a case about it, but we've got match racing calls about it. The match racing call says that the leeward boat can luff, but at the point where the windward boat's gennaker ceases to draw, the leeward boat has then got to give some extra room for the windward boat to drop the gennaker. If the windward boat drops her gennaker then the leeward boat can continue to luff. If the windward boat, having been given the room, does not drop the gennaker, the leeward boat can also continue to luff without making any extra allowance. And I think it's the same here, so the leeward boat can certainly luff until the windward boat's gennaker is flapping. At that stage she must make sure that there is sufficient room for the windward boat to take down the gennaker if that's what she wants to do (which might be quite a substantial course change for a single-hander with a gennaker). But I suspect, in most asymmetric boats, by the time it gets to that point, the leeward boat will have moved ahead of the windward boat anyway."

HANDICAP RACING – DIFFERENT BOATS AT THE SAME MARK

Q In handicap racing, with boats of different speeds and sizes competing against each other, tell us about the rights and wrongs of a scenario where, say, an 18-foot Skiff is closing rapidly on a mark where a 10-foot Mirror dinghy is about to enter the three boat-length zone. How is the size of the boat-length zone defined, for example?

ANSWER: *"The zone is defined as the area around the mark within a distance of three hull lengths of the boat nearer to it. So, if a slow Mirror is approaching a mark, the zone is three Mirror hull lengths because the Mirror is the boat that's closer. As soon as the longer boat – in this case the 18-foot Skiff – gets ahead, the zone is three of her hull lengths. So they go from not being in the zone of the short boat to instantaneously being well inside the zone of the long boat. Because there was no point at which they 'reach' the zone (they instantaneously became within it when the long boat got ahead) we do not have that reference point to use rule 18.2(b) – so the basic rule 18.2(a) applies and the outside boat must give the inside boat mark-room."*

BOWSPRIT IN 'NORMAL POSITION'

Q How does having a bowsprit extended out of the front of the boat affect overlaps for rules situations?

ANSWER: *"An overlap is determined by equipment in normal position. The definition says that one boat is clear astern of another when her hull and equipment in normal position are behind a line abeam of the aftermost point of the other boat's hull and equipment in normal position. So if we think of two International 14s approaching a windward mark and one boat is clear of astern of the other. If the boat astern then pulls out her bowsprit she doesn't create an overlap because having your bowsprit out on an upwind leg is not equipment in normal position."*

GYBING A FULLY-BATTENED MAINSAIL WITHOUT UPSETTING THE UMPIRES

Q In light winds, gybing a fully-battened mainsail such as you have on the majority of asymmetric boats can be quite difficult, because it can be hard convincing the battens to flick from one gybe to another. From a rules perspective, what sort of things do sailors need to be aware of when they're gybing the battens on their sail?

ANSWER: *"It is a matter of whether the tug on the mainsheet clearly propels the boat or not. If, in attempting to gybe the battens, there is a quick flick so that the boom doesn't move significantly and all that happens is that the battens flip across up the sail, then that does not have any effect, or its effect is negligible. So it doesn't break the rule.*

On the other hand, if the pull on the mainsheet moves the boom a significant amount, and the whole sail moves as well – the fact that the battens pop across in the course of that happening would not exonerate you from pumping if it had an effect on the boat."

No matter what level you're at, there is always room for improvement. In this chapter we'll look at how to make those crucial, incremental improvements to your boat, your equipment, and yourself. Small changes can make massive differences to your results, and the most successful sailors are those that pay the most attention to the tiniest details.

PERFECTING YOUR EQUIPMENT

It would be easy to write a whole book on this subject. Instead we'll focus on a few key points.

The main point to bear in mind is that attention to detail makes a massive difference in high-performance boats. When you're juggling the tiller, mainsheet, kite sheets all while balancing on the edge of the boat on the trapeze, the last thing you want to have to cope with is a cleat that won't hold the sheet properly or anything else that distracts you from actually sailing the boat. Small things can lead to a capsize, and a capsize can lead to gear damage. So pay attention to the details.

The best place to start is to look at the National Champion's boat, or the most competent sailor in your local fleet. With their permission, copy their rope lengths and anything else that you see done differently on their boat.

Here are a few examples of things that might help improve the smooth running of your boat:

- **Tapered gennaker halyard:** The only bit of the halyard that needs to be thick is the bit you hold during the hoist. Everything else can be as thin as possible for the given strength required. On a 49er, for example, you might have 3mm spectra from the head of the kite all the way to where it's about to go into the halyard cleat. From this point on it can thicken

out to 5mm, good for gripping the cleat and good for gripping with your hands.

- **Loop on the gennaker sheet:** Instead of tying your gennaker sheets on to the clew of the kite with separate knots, use a loop in

The kite sheets (top) could catch on the forestay during a gybe, whereas the smooth run on the sheets (bottom) will make a more reliable gybe

the centre of the sheets, creating a smooth run past the forestay. Anything you can do to reduce friction as the kite goes through the gybe will help speed up the manoeuvre.

- **Tapered kite sheets:** These can help the kite set more easily in light winds, weighing down the clew less than if you use thick, non-tapered sheets.
- **Lubricating spray:** Spray anywhere on the boat where you want to reduce unwanted friction. I use McLube but there are other brands available. It's not cheap, but spraying the chute mouth, the bowsprit and other parts of the hoist system can make it much easier to get the kite up and down. Just make sure you don't spray the parts of the boat where you're going to be treading, because these lube sprays can be superslippery underfoot.

Lubricating spray to reduce friction in the gennaker hoist system and chute

- **Vital spares**: Always take a few spare shackles, pieces of string and other things that you might need in an emergency. For trapeze boats, think about taking a spare tiller extension with you. If you break one, you'll certainly struggle to continue racing without it, and it might make it difficult to get home safely. Carbon tiller extensions weigh very little, so it's worth the small weight penalty for the added peace of mind.

HOW OFTEN TO A BUY NEW KITE?

On a lot of asymmetric boats, gennakers don't really get much slower as they get older. At least not in a straight line. But, over time, as the cloth loses its shiny, water-resistant coating, and becomes porous and prone to soaking up water, you'll find it becomes harder to handle through the manoeuvres. The kite might stick to the jib through gybes or get a lot harder to hoist and drop into the chute. When to buy a replacement kite really depends on how much your manoeuvres are being affected by your old kite. Really high-performance asymmetrics with tight-luffed gennakers need to replace their sails more often as the shape becomes distorted, but for lower-performance asymmetrics, a new kite should last you for a year's worth of weekend racing.

TEAMWORK & COMMUNICATION

One of the hardest things to get right in high-performance sailing boats is efficient communication and understanding between the crew. Because the boat is demanding to sail and it travels at a rapid rate, typically around a short course, the decision making comes thick and fast.

Practise your set moves and build up a few standard forms of communication so that you can reduce chatter to a minimum. The fastest boats also tend to be the quietest. Calibrate sail controls so that you can make adjustments with the minimum of guess work. Instead of saying 'ease the vang a bit', it's a lot easier for everyone to understand

Iker Martinez and Xabi Fernandez sailed as a team together for years, a major contributing factor to their Olympic and World titles in the 49er, as well as their offshore success in round-the-world races too

'ease the vang to 4', for example.

When your crew mate isn't quite doing what you want them to do, say, maybe they're standing too far forwards, choose your words carefully. Tell them what you want, not what you don't want. Instead of saying, 'You're standing too far forwards', give them a more specific instruction like 'Step back 15cm (six inches)'.

These things are hard to get right straight away, but the important thing is to agree to offer each other constructive feedback on what each of you think is working, and what could be done better. Try not to get stuck into making too many corrections at once, or during an already busy sailing session, but remember the main points and discuss them in a debrief once you're back on shore.

EXPERT ADVICE

Frances Peters: Who makes the decisions?

ISAF Youth Champion in the 29er skiff, Frances Peters answers my questions about tactical decision-making in the team.

 Frances, what's the main difference in communication style between racing a slower boat and a faster asymmetric skiff like the 29er?

ANSWER: *"One of the biggest transitions probably was the amount of communication needed from the crew downwind, to constantly be feeding back how much pressure they have in the kite. This feedback enables the helm to ease the boat down every wave, as low as they can get without losing pressure in the gennaker completely. That was a big transition and really important in team building of course, because the communication is absolutely vital."*

 What about the split of responsibilities downwind? Who's calling the tactics, for example?

ANSWER: *"I think tactics is the helm's job. It's really important that the crew focuses entirely on the kite because their job downwind is to make sure that the kite stays filling, feeding back how much pressure they've got in the kite and possibly helping with pumping and ooching down the waves. The helm is responding to the feedback they're getting from the crew and they're looking around, calling in the pressure, calling in where the other boats are and generally doing all the tactics and strategy."*

 One of the toughest parts of the course is the leeward gate, where the decision-making process can change depending on what's going on around you. How do you manage that, and communicate your plans to the crew?

ANSWER: *"Well, just talk lots! Don't try to tell them what's going on I'd say, because you generally haven't got time to do that, so you've just got to make sure that you tell them what to do with as much opportunity as possible. Coming into a gate mark I generally try to say in advance, 'okay, it's going to be a gybe-drop here', for example, and my crew will instantly know what that means and what that entails. I'll try to give them an idea of what I think the situation will be but, as you say, situations do change. In which case I'd say it's the crew's responsibility to keep up with the helm and it's the helm's responsibility to feed in as much information as they possibly can and give the crew time. You can't afford to be vague and you can't afford to assume that the crew knows what's going on. It's about teamwork, it's lots of practice. Whatever call you make in any situation, both of you have to know what's involved because you've practised it so many times before."*

With the crew focused on kite trim, tactical decisions downwind should be taken by the helm

GOAL SETTING – DO THIS & YOU WILL ALWAYS IMPROVE

I wrote this section in conjunction with **Richard Parslow**, *a World Champion sailor and my former RYA coach when I was racing the 49er.*

Of all the things that full-time, professional sailors do that the rest of us weekend warriors do not do, structured goal setting is probably the most important. Fortunately, it is also one of the less demanding activities (compared to, say, completing a hundred perfect tacks). With the right approach it can be done quickly – and it can even be fun.

WHY GOAL SETTING MAKES A DIFFERENCE

It's not just about the time and money (and energy!) you have available, it's how you spend those resources. For example, practising some boat-handling exercises might be a better use of a day's sailing than doing a couple of club races. Or maybe a day's coaching is a better investment than buying a new jib.

Think about what you want to achieve, then set some specific goals. Goal setting has been shown to be a major factor in improving performance in almost every area of life; yet most of us still do not set any goals, let alone reach them. Maybe we are protecting ourselves: if we do not set goals, we cannot fail at them! But that is lazy thinking, and it brings only frustration.

So let's look at setting some sailing goals – and working out how to achieve them.

MAPPING OUT YOUR ROAD TO SUCCESS

Think about your long-term sailing goals. How exactly do you want to improve? What specific goal will motivate you to do everything you need to do to achieve it? Maybe you want to be so fit and skilled that you are 'at one with your boat' in all conditions; or maybe you just want to be able to compete in 25 knots without capsizing.

Try to stick to **Performance** and **Process** goals: those that depend entirely on your own efforts and abilities. You can set **Outcome** goals: winning a club series or a championship – or even an Olympic medal, but you have to accept that achieving such goals is not completely within your control.

You want to improve as much as possible with the talent, time and money you bring to the game, so aim high. Describe your goal in inspirational terms and write it down somewhere as your Main Goal. Once you know where you are going, you can start to work out how to get there. What's most important in the goal-setting process is the journey you take to reach the desired outcome.

You can do quite a lot on paper – as long as you keep it somewhere safe and easily accessible. I use Goalscape software (www.goalscape.com) because it can capture an entire campaign in a single picture – and because it's really easy to use.

Lots of sailors in Olympic classes use this tool, but it can help anyone who is serious about improving their skills – and results.

NEXT YEAR'S RESULTS DEPEND ON WHAT YOU DO RIGHT NOW

The best way to plan your route to your main goal is to break down your sailing into different areas and work out exactly what you need to do in each.

The fundamental 'building blocks' are always the same, whatever your current abilities and whatever your goals. In the diagram below you can see the top-level sub-goals around the main goal in the centre. (The size of each sub-goal's slice represents its relative importance.)

Three of these goals are about arriving at the starting line in the best possible shape:

1. Logistics (planning the year: training, events, travel and accommodation, etc.)
2. Gear (hull, rig, sails, foils, fittings, clothing, etc.)
3. Budget (money available for equipment, events etc.)

These goals are all about preparation. You can start thinking right now about what you need to do and how to do it.

The other three are about the abilities you need when racing:

1. Boat handling (executing every skill in all conditions)
2. Finding the best course (strategy and tactics)
3. Fitness (mental skills, physical strength, balance, etc.)

These are the core goals for maximising your performance on the water.

Define specific goals in each area and plan exactly how you are going to achieve them. Break down each sub-goal area into further sub-goals.

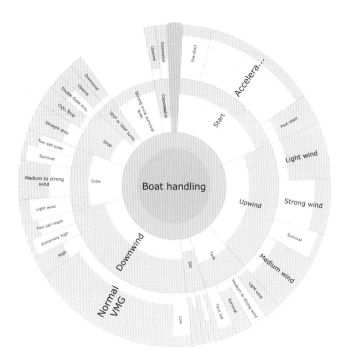

Keep breaking down the sub-goals even further until you have defined specific actions to achieve them all. Above is a detail view of the 'Boat handling' area, showing the key aspects of boat handling that you need to master in order to race properly and the specific manoeuvres involved.

FOCUS YOUR EFFORTS

When you first do a proper goal-setting exercise, it can be exciting when you see all the different areas where you can improve. It can also be overwhelming! A common mistake here is to go from doing nothing to trying to do too much all at once.

A good way to start is to identify a maximum of three areas that offer the greatest opportunity for improving your performance. How do you do that? One way is to think back through your last season, or even your last race. Be honest: what did you do well and what let you down? Where could you make the greatest improvements in the shortest time? If you capsized a lot when tacking in strong winds for example, you have an easy answer.

So if you can come up with three ideas for tacking more safely, then you can write them into your tacking process breakdown as sub-goals:

1. Ease sails sooner before the tack
2. Steer more slowly through the tack
3. Move more quickly up to the new windward side

Work out some good ways to practise and how to measure your progress. If you train in a pair or a group, watch what the others do. Ask them to watch you and give you some specific feedback.

On the other hand, if your boat handling is good but your race strategy is poor, look at your information gathering and decision-making processes.

Find out how other people do all this stuff: talk to some of the good guys – or visit a sailing forum. Debrief thoroughly after each practice or competition. Be positive: agree where you have improved and how much. Update your written plan – seeing your progress increases your motivation and highlights what you need to prioritise next.

If you identify specific problems in every area and find three possible solutions for each of them (or just one!), you are already doing better than 95% of your opposition.

STICK AT IT!

Persist with this process of gradual, incremental improvements to the key areas of your game and your weaknesses will start to disappear. You may find that your old failings become your new strengths: each is a separate proof of the effectiveness of your process.

Soon you will enjoy doing the very things that you used to mess up. If you were nervous in strong winds you will be more competent and more confident: you will love racing in a breeze when you can stay upright while your rivals are falling over.

Double Olympic Champion Iain Percy once said: *"I enjoy the process of improvement almost more than the winning itself. That's where the real satisfaction comes. Identify your weaknesses, set goals, practise until you get better, and the results will look after themselves."*

So, start setting some goals for your sailing right now. It is the single activity most likely to improve your performance and results; there is simply no excuse not to do it. And don't stop goal setting even if you reach your goals – in fact especially if you reach your goals. Instead, set yourself new goals in every area – and start working on them today.

PART 3

121

The author leading a race at the National Championships in his Musto Skiff

PHOTOGRAPHERS

Thanks to the photographers and organisations who were kind enough to allow the use of their work for this book.

Jeremy Atkins, for the RS200 & RS800 photos from Lymington
Mark Barnes for his B14 on-the-water videos from which we have extracted some stills
GBR International 14 Class, with special thanks to Andrew Penman (gbr.international14.org)
Tom Gruitt for the photo on page 101
Natalie Hilton, for her Musto Skiff photos
LPB Aerial Imagery for the photos on pages 12 & 91
Paul Manning, for photos from the archive of the Musto Skiff Class Association (www.mustoskiff.com)
Tim Olin for the cover photo and the photo on page 121
Chris Simon, for his brilliant illustrations for the Rules chapter

THANKS FOR THE BOATS

Alice Moore for the loan of her RS200 for a photoshoot at my sailing club, Stokes Bay Sailing Club.
Derek Clark for driving the photo boat and the loan of his Rebel Skiff, and to Andy Budgen, Dave Hivey and Mari Shepherd for getting very wet in the making of those photos.

Emma and Luke McEwen for their RS800 and Jeremy and Maxine Vines for their RS200 for the photoshoot at Royal Lymington Yacht Club. Andrew Eady for driving the RIB, Emma and Luke for sailing their RS800 and Emma Porteous and Tristan Jaques for sailing the RS200.

ROAD TO GOLD

YOUR 12-STEP PLAN FOR A WORLD-BEATING SAILING CAMPAIGN

Three-time 470 World Champion Hamish Willcox has coached many sailors to Olympic and America's Cup glory over the past 30 years. Working in partnership with the author of *The Asymmetric Dinghy Book*, Andy Rice, Willcox shares his 12-module battle-proven Blueprint on how to put together a World Class Sailing Campaign.

It's called Road To Gold. It works at all levels of the sport, from club racer to aspiring Olympic medallist.

To find out more and download an ebook explaining the principles behind this world-beating system, get your free PDF download here:

www.roadtogold.net/p/asymmbook

© Sailing Energy/ World Sailing: Hamish Willcox celebrates 49er Olympic Gold with Pete Burling and Blair Tuke

SAIL TO WIN

Taking a fresh look at the complex subject of racing to get you moving up the leaderboard

6

View our entire list at **www.fernhurstbooks.com**

Sign up to receive details of new books & exclusive special offers at
www.fernhurstbooks.com/register

Get to know us more on **social media**

FERNHURST BOOKS

CHAPTER 1
Pre-Start

BASIC PREPARATIONS (BEGINNER)

Before you even decide to enter the race / regatta, make sure you are properly prepared. How long does it take to the venue? (Giving you enough rest.) Have you sorted out good accommodation? When do you need to enter? (Many regattas implement a surcharge if you enter late, so make your mind up!) Is your boat race-ready and do you have all the spares you need?

Read the sailing instructions so you know the course you are racing, where it is and when; and don't forget to check the official notice board for changes to the SIs (sailing instructions) as it is not uncommon for amendments to be made. World Championships have been won and lost when people didn't notice a change of start time.

Races can be decided before the warning signal is even blown. Establish what the most important tactic(s) will be for the day. Get the big things sorted (like not over-standing the layline with strong current under you) before you worry about the little things (a small amount of dirty air).

You need to break things down so, first of all, consider the variables that will affect the course you would sail in the absence of other boats.

Current

A strong favourable current (or less adverse current) on one side of the course may be the most important factor, especially with slower moving boats. You can check the current by placing a 2/3 full bottle of liquid by a mark and seeing how far it moves in a minute. (Pick it up afterwards.)

If the wind is offshore, you can check the current on your sail out to the start line. Launch early to give yourself plenty of time.

Charlie Current is always keen to maximise his tidal advantage compared to other boats

Windshifts / Bends

If there is a big shift, getting to it first can make a real difference. You may be expecting this windshift because of a weather forecast or, if the wind is stable, you may see the shift affecting boats further to windward or there may be a wind bend due to the shore line.

Sally Shift is always keen to maximise the gain of an expected big shift

Sally Shift also likes to maximise the gain from an expected wind bend

Get out on the race course early – the precise placement of the race course will affect your tactics. (The exact position of the racing area should be given in the Sailing Instructions.) If there is an oscillating breeze, try to get in tune with it (work out the frequency and duration). If not just practise your tacking!!

Terry Tacker likes to tack in a shifting breeze

Terry Tacker also likes to gain by tacking in an oscillating breeze

Wind Speed / Pressure

With a big difference in wind speed, the windier side of the course may be heavily favoured, especially with boats which beat upwind.

More wind makes the water look darker so, when an area of the water is dark, there is more wind there. Where there are more white horses there is also more wind than in the flatter areas (assuming no current difference).

In light winds (under 7 knots) even a small difference in wind speed (say 4-6 knots) can make a big difference in boatspeed.

If the breeze is offshore, you can probably work out which is the windiest part of the race course on the way to the start line.

Reaching Hoist, Leeward Bag

In preparation, pull out some of the guy, helm puts on the twinner

Come off the trapeze on the bear away

Unhook from the trapeze

Attach the guy to the pole, call '1'

Attach the uphaul to the pole, call '2'; the helm will start to hoist

Push the pole out as the helm hoists

Attach the pole to the mast

Grab the sheet

Get the spinnaker filling

Reaching Hoist, Leeward Bag

This is the basic hoist, which you will set up for pre-start assuming you are doing a port rounding at the top. Ideally you will have had a starboard tack approach to the windward mark.

• On your final port approach, check the halyard is clear of the end of the spreaders.
• On your final starboard approach pull the clew of the kite out of the bag, get your helm to pull the twinner on to mark (pre-start - always do a practice hoist so you know where this is and it gives you the chance to leave a tail on the spinnaker sheet if it is too long).
• As you bear away, trim the jib. If you are over max power, let the helm get settled in terms of centreboard and kicker and come in on their call. They will match any further bear away to you coming in. If you can raise your trapeze hook in this process it will make getting it on post hoist easier, but don't waste any time on it. If you are under max power, go straight for the pole.
• As soon as you are off the wire, you are down power and anyone who does this quicker than you is back up to speed faster: SO MAKE IT HAPPEN!
• Feed the pole out under the jibsheet, straight onto the guy (call '1'), middle pole hook on (call '2', which is when the helm can go for the halyard to hoist) and open the mast. If it's windy getting it on to the mast might be difficult. Get a stable base with your legs so the spinnaker's flapping doesn't boss you around, deep breath and get it done.
• From here it will be a race to the spinnaker sheet between you and your helm. If the wind is light enough you can have the sheet cleated in the port cleat tidy in the boat, so the spinnaker will automatically be sheeted, but make sure this in uncleated during your preparation if it is windier.
• As soon as you have the spinnaker sheet do whatever is needed for optimum boat heel.

This might be staying down to leeward and generating some heel or, if it's windier, grab the trapeze handle and power out on to the windward side as you go, as you are likely to be over-sheeted. If you managed to get your trapeze hook height up a bit on the bear away then you can go straight onto the hook, otherwise get your helm to hook you on or take the spinnaker sheet whilst you hook on.

Reaching Hoist, Windward Bag

This can be hugely costly in terms of tactical positioning during a race, so it is worth spending some time getting your process right because sometimes it will be unavoidable.

There are 2 ways:

1. 'Chuck it'

There is no preparation to do, you can't have the twinner pre-cleated as it will restrict the throw and risk the spinnaker not getting around the forestay.

• Bear away as before, come in on your helm's call keeping as much height as you can.
• Clear the halyard from the spreader.
• Gather up the kite out of the bag cleanly in a ball and be careful not to put any twists in it. You need to be max forward, next to the mast so the windward shroud doesn't get in your way when you go for the chuck.
• On your call, launch the kite ('2', '1', 'Go') with the focus on looping it round the forestay, not giving it height. On the shout of 'Go' the helm will hoist.
• Go straight to the twinner and then the pole as before. The helm will definitely beat you to the sheet.

The 'chuck it' definitely has a maximum wind strength above which it won't work and the spinnaker will just get blown back in your face. In that scenario you need to go for the big bear away (see p66).

FERNHURST
BOOKS

We hope you enjoyed this book

If you did, **please post a review on Amazon**